A Digital Design Methodology
for Optical Computing

A Digital Design Methodology for Optical Computing

Miles Murdocca

The MIT Press
Cambridge, Massachusetts
London, England

This book was set in Times Roman.
Printed and bound in the United States of America.

Library of Congress Cataloging-in-Publication Data

Murdocca, Miles.
    A digital design methodology for optical computing / Miles Murdocca.
        p.   cm.
    Includes bibliographical references.
    ISBN 0-262-13251-6
    1. Optical data processing. 2. Computers, Optical. 3. Digital integrated circuits. I. Title.
    TA1630.M87 1990   90-5480
    621.39'1—dc20   CIP

Contents

Preface

Nearly half of the content of this book comes from my Rutgers doctoral dissertation. My original intent was that this book should be an expanded Ph.D. thesis in the form of a monograph that promotes the message: "Use regular free-space interconnects for optical computing." My aim was to help steer the field of optical computing in this direction by providing convincing arguments that complicated, exotic means for interconnecting optical logic gates are unwarranted. That's the purpose of a monograph – a narrow, deep expository on a single subject. I'm grateful to the reviewers who convinced me to make it into the broader book you are now reading, because the interested reader hopes to gain more than a single insight from a book dealing with such a new technology.

The intended audience for this book includes computer engineers, computer scientists, physicists, and other scientists who have an interest in digital optical computing. This book is written from the perspective of a computer designer, with an emphasis on a design methodology that simplifies the optical hardware without adding complexity to the design process. I have done my best to include other approaches to general purpose digital optical design that cover the more celebrated areas of research such as hybrid optical/electronic approaches and guided wave interconnects. Unlike the Feitelson survey *Optical Computing* (The MIT Press, 1988) which gives an overview of the field, I have presented the material in this text with distinct biases toward regularity in design and simplicity in methods. I argue against methods that introduce complexity in the optical hardware or add difficulty to the design process. My position is that high performance computers *in any technology* must exhibit regularity in structure and must submit to simple design techniques. This must be the case if our goal is to manage the enormous complexity of next-generation computers.

Inspiration is not born in a vacuum. The reader should not pore over the text and gaze at the figures in amazement that a single mind could have dreamed up such wonders. It didn't. Two years after I joined AT&T Bell Laboratories, the world's largest corporation divested itself and entered an age of competition in the long distance telecommunications market. The climate within AT&T changed from benevolent monopoly to market-driven competitor. That might have been the case for the whole company, but efforts were made to protect the research area from the front lines. Optical computing took the limelight as an example that Bell Labs research still thrived, and enjoyed considerable support. I've been lucky to have been involved with optical computing at this time, enjoying the freedom of exploring my own interests in optical computing while enjoying interaction with the development side of the business. The interaction between research and development at Bell Labs fostered a sense of direction and purpose that I feel has led the frontier in optical computing technology. Part of the culture of research at Bell Labs is the maintenance of an academic atmosphere. Some people joke that their real employer is The Institute of Electrical and Electronics Engineers (IEEE), a scientific organization that publishes professional journals and sponsors technical meetings. A result of this thinking is a visible presence at professional meetings, through which I am grateful to have met many of the inventors at other institutions whose works are cited in this text.

In the last few years, the Air Force Office of Scientific Research (AFOSR) funded a startup project at Rutgers exploring the application of digital optical computing to large structured problems like content addressable memory (CAM). My involvement with the Rutgers group allowed me to make greater progress toward the ideas presented in this book than if my time was divided among many areas of research. The Rutgers group identified problems with electronic systems that led to the optical content addressable memory (CAM) and Connection Machine case studies described in Chapter 5. The Rutgers AFOSR sponsored project maintained ties with the Bell Labs groups which allowed large architectural problems to be studied at Rutgers without taking on the additional burden of building the optical hardware.

The text is organized into six chapters that should be read in order. The first chapter provides motivations for using optics in digital computing, and gives a brief history of the field. The breadth of coverage is incomplete with respect to the field as a whole and is biased toward the methodology supported in this text, and I refer the reader to Feitelson's survey for a more complete background. I don't think there is enough breadth to teach an entire course from this text, although it would make a good supplemental text for a VLSI design course, a seminar on advanced computer architectures, or a broader course on optical computing.

The status of optical hardware discussed in Chapter 2 is a moving target because advances are made on a daily basis. A few trends noted in the chapter are not likely to grow obsolete so quickly however, such as the fabrication of regular arrays of identical logic gates and the need for small, easily manufacturable optical systems. Issues are treated in a topical manner because I don't want to lessen the emphasis on regularity in design and simplicity in methods by providing distractions on device specifics that may have little relevance in a few years.

Chapter 3 describes alternative approaches to designing a general purpose digital optical computer and introduces the reader to the main approach described in Chapter 4, which is the methodology supported in this book. The approaches discussed are representative of current work going on in the field but are by no means complete. I don't want to confound or distract the reader by offering too much information, rather, my intent is to expose the reader to enough material to appreciate the methodology presented in Chapter 4.

Chapter 4 is the monograph that was all this book was originally intended to be, the presentation of a methodology of designing digital circuits for an optical computer. This is the backbone of the text, that shows how to design regularity into digital optical circuits with simple methods, that yield high performance without introducing significant complexity into the target machine. One of the discussions offers a profound capability that regular free-space interconnects afford us, which is the ability to completely reconfigure the gate-to-gate interconnects of a computer on every time step, at little additional hardware cost. How do we exploit the potential of such a machine? This chapter stands apart from the rest of the text in describing a complete methodology for designing digital optical circuits, and can serve as a good complement to a conventional digital design course dealing with advanced architectures.

Chapter 5 describes three case studies designed with the approach presented in Chapter 4. A parallel sorting network design makes a particularly strong case for regularity. The Rutgers CAM and optical Connection Machine case studies support this methodology by overcoming the pinout and other input/output (I/O) constraints of conventional Very Large Scale Integration (VLSI).

Chapter 6 touches on some philosophical issues of computing, such as why it is desirable to create more powerful computers. A brief summary reinforces the ideas discussed in earlier chapters.

I have found that clarity is the most gifted tool a technical writer may possess. Acronyms are only used in this book when they have been clearly defined in other published literature; I have created no new acronyms in this text, and I have defined all old acronyms on their first use and also on subsequent uses if a sizeable lapse occurs between uses. In the interest of promoting current writing style, I have referred to all persons with genderless words except where the gender of a person is commonly known and pertinent to the discussion. I have avoided using words that are overly colorful or unusual so that the reader can move quickly through the text without stumbling over words. I hope that my efforts at writing simply and clearly for the reader's benefit are successful.

Miles Murdocca
AT&T Bell Laboratories
Holmdel, New Jersey
and
Rutgers University
New Brunswick, New Jersey

Acknowledgements

I couldn't have done this work alone, and I gratefully acknowledge the support of many people and institutions for their influence in my thinking and in the preparation of this book. Those supporters, listed alphabetically, are: The Air Force Office of Scientific Research, Ravi Athale, AT&T Bell Laboratories, Karl-Heinz Brenner, Ike Chuang, Tom Cloonan, Nick Craft, Alex Dickinson, Maralene Downs, Chris Gabriel, Lee Giles, John Storrs Hall, Alan Huang, Jürgen Jahns, Scott Knauer, Vijay Kumar, Yong Lee, Tony Lentine, Saul Levy, Haw-Minn Lu, my parents Dolores and Nicholas Murdocca, Bob Prior and The MIT Press, Irv Rabinowitz, the Rutgers Computer Science Department, Tod Sizer, Lou Steinberg, Charlie Stirk, Norbert Streibl, Binay Sugla, Tony Terrano, Stu Tewksbury, Sue Walker, Larry West, all of the people who acted as readers of early drafts, and Jack Jewell, Mike Prise, Rick McCormick, and Norm Whitaker for not leaving me stranded in the Grand Canyon, and to the unnamed hiker who pointed us to the right trail when Norm and I were blustering up the wrong one a few hours before my talk in Nevada.

There are surely other people and institutions who have contributed to this book, either directly or indirectly, whose names I have inadvertently omitted. To those people and institutions I offer my tacit appreciation and apologize for having omitted explicit recognition here.

I think I had it easier than most, with the support of my employer, my school, my family, and especially my wife Ellen, who has watched me sit in front of this silly computer every day and night in amazement that anyone would do it by choice. For your patience and encouragement, this is for you Ellen.

A Digital Design Methodology
for Optical Computing

Chapter 1
Introduction

There are rewards in building regularity into complex systems that are appreciated only after time has passed and the systems approach maturity. For example, consider the difference in street layouts of Boston and New York. Boston started out as a relatively small town that grew in incremental steps to become a metropolitan center of the northeastern United States, with a seemingly spaghetti-like system of roads that confounds the passing automobile driver. People familiar with Boston sometimes say: "If you don't know where you are driving in Boston, then don't drive in Boston." New York City on the other hand, with a grid-like road system over most of Manhattan is more easily navigated by the common driver, and local eddies are more easily smoothed with traffic light synchronization that adjusts for changing volume. Regularities are most appreciated when looking back at systems that grow to great sizes without choking from their masses.

Optics can improve regularity in computer design but it may not be obvious at first why a light based technology should have an advantage over an electronics based technology. After all, light and electricity both travel at the speed of light so we can't expect an optical computer to run any faster than an electronic computer, unless there are some limiting problems inherent in one technology that are not inherent in the other. That is the case as will be discussed in the next section, and the key to these ideas is *regularity*.

1.1 Why optical computing?

We should consider that there is a large disparity between the speed of the fastest electronic switching components and the speed of the fastest digital electronic computers. Figure 1.1 illustrates the problem, in showing that transistors exist that can switch in 5ps while the fastest computers run at clock rates on the order of a few nanoseconds. What are the causes of this slowdown for increasing hardware complexity, and how can we get the system speeds closer to the device speeds?

Transistor	5ps
Ring oscillator	30ps
Logic gate	120ps
Chip	1ns
System	5ns

Figure 1.1: *The difference in speed between one of the fastest transistors and one of the fastest computers is a factor of ~1000. (Table provided by the courtesy of Alan Huang, AT&T Bell Laboratories.)*

Limitations of electronics, which is the contending technology for interconnection at this time, include [66]:

- Electromagnetic interference at high speed
- Distorted edge transitions
- Complexity of metal connections
- Drive requirements for pins
- Large peak power levels
- Impedance matching effects

Electromagnetic interference arises because the inductances of two current carrying wires are coupled. Sharp edge transitions must be maintained for proper switching but higher frequencies are attenuated greater than lower frequencies, resulting in sloppy edges at high speeds. The complexity of metal connections on chips, on circuit boards, and between system components affects connection topology and introduces complex fields and unequal path lengths. This translates to signal skews that are overcome by slowing the system clock rate so that signals overlap sufficiently in time. Large peak power levels are needed to overcome residual capacitances, and impedance matching effects at connections require high currents which result in lower system speeds.

Guided wave methods suffer from none of the disadvantages of electronics mentioned here so they are gaining acceptance in large systems such as AT&T's

5ESS [2] central office switch. However, topological complexity introduced by bending tolerances for fibers, volume requirements, and skew effects pose serious enough limitations to preclude the use of guided wave technology for complex gate-level interconnects, unless radical improvements to the technology are made.

A technology based on optics offers solutions to these problems if we can exploit the advantages of optics without introducing new complexity or new limitations that render the use of optics ineffective. Advantages of using free-space optics for interconnection include [66]:

- High connectivity through imaging
- No physical contact for interconnects
- Non-interference of signals
- High spatial and temporal bandwidth
- No feedback to the power source
- Inherently low signal dispersion

High connectivity can be achieved by imaging a large array of light beams onto an array of optical logic devices. There is no need for physical interconnects (unless fibers or waveguides are used) so that connection complexity is simplified and drive requirements are reduced. Optical signals do not interact in free space, which means that beams can pass right through each other without interference. This allows for a high density of signals in a small volume. High bandwidth is achieved in space because of the non-interference property of optical signals, and high bandwidth is achieved in time because propagating wavefronts do not interact. There is no feedback to the power source as in electronics, so that there are no data dependent loads. Finally, inherently low signal dispersion means that the shape of a pulse as it leaves it source is virtually unchanged when it reaches its destination.

From the viewpoint of a computer designer, probably the single most significant advantage of optics over electronics is *communication*. Optical logic gates can be oriented normal to the surface of an optical chip so that light beams travel in parallel between arrays of optical logic devices rather than through pins at the edges of chips as in electronic integrated circuits (ICs) as illustrated in Figure 1.2.

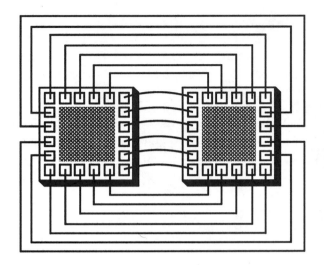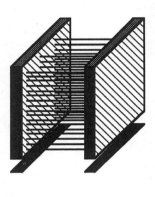

Figure 1.2: *Edge connections between electronic chips (left) and parallel connections between optical chips (right).*

Free-space storage, lack of signal skew, and dense communication are just a few of the properties of free-space optics that can be exploited in the implementation of a digital computer. A wired approach or a guided wave approach for interconnection in an advanced architecture can quickly dominate the cost of the entire machine and can pose the most serious speed limitation. Irregular free-space interconnects reduce spatial bandwidth (the amount of information that can be passed through a lens) in holographic implementations because a minimum spacing must be maintained in the input plane to avoid crosstalk in the output plane. The use of regular free-space interconnects allows the entire chip area to be devoted to active switching rather than to communication. Device failure is not nearly as critical because circuits can be redesigned after the positions of faulty components are known. Thus a free-space approach to interconnection offers significant advantages over other means of interconnection.

There are limits imposed by the methods supported in this book. Strictly speaking, electronics is not worse than optics for short distance communication, on the order of a centimeter. Photons do not interact with other photons directly, and typically involve electrons even in an "all-optical" approach, and this conversion between electrons and photons consumes time and energy. Electronics is a mature, inexpensive technology that allows for a high density of switching components. Photonics on the other hand is less mature and requires tight imaging tolerances and constant power consumption for modulator-based optical logic gates. The position is argued here that an all-optical computer will result in a simpler design than a hybrid optical/electronic approach, and that this simplicity is more significant for managing complexity in digital optical computing than an inherent superiority at the quantum level. Still, the reader should be mindful of the advantages of electronic digital computing, and that nearly five decades of electronic technology should not be completely cast aside.

Another limitation of the optical approach described in the rest of this book is that optical logic gates are spaced a few microns apart on optical chips but require several hundreds of microns, and possibly several centimeters of interaction distance for lenses, gratings, and other imaging components. The use of microoptic techniques (monolithically fabricated lenses) can be applied to reduce or eliminate this problem but for initial systems an infant technology like microoptics should not be relied upon as the basis for connections. This means that switching speeds on the order of 100ps or faster cannot be exploited in a tight feedback loop because the interaction distance forces a minimum separation between arrays of devices. Fast switching speeds can still be accommodated because free space can provide a delay memory allowing propagating wavefronts of information to be maintained between arrays. In a pipelined system, this minimum separation is not significant when the pipeline remains filled. Applications that can take advantage of the bandwidth and parallelism of free-space propagation without suffering from the minimum device separation along the propagation axis include signal processing, digital switching (as in a telephone central office switch), and matrix-vector multiplication. If microoptic techniques mature to accommodate the free-space interconnection needs of the systems described here, then the applications that digital optical systems are suited for can broaden to include nearly every application that is limited by speed or connectivity.

In consideration of these arguments we might conclude that optics is a better technology for digital computing, but we need to support this claim by showing how to apply this technology to an entire system, and measure the cost and performance of the system that results. The chapters that follow give more specific evidence that regularity in structure and simplicity in design methods are suitable goals for digital optical computing by showing how such a machine can be constructed and what new advantages can be exploited.

1.2 A brief history of optical computing

Digital computing with the use of optical components was considered at least as early as the 1940's by von Neumann [118]. If lasers were available at the time, the first digital computers may well have used optics. In the early 1960's and throughout the 1970's and 1980's, optics technology was employed for computing Fourier transforms of military images in matched filtering operations. Synthetic aperture radar (SAR) signal processing [19, 34, 40] matches images in stored photographic form with input images, at a very high rate. Spectrum analysis is performed with acousto-optic signal processing [102]. Both of these applications are performed optically when bandwidth needs exceed electronic capability.

Studies at IBM [69] showed that digital optics would not surpass digital electronics with technology available in the foreseeable future, and arguments in favor of optical computing were hard to support except in a few niche applications like matched filtering. There were renewed interests in the late 1970's as advances were made in optical transmission and optically nonlinear materials. Limits of electronic digital circuits became more apparent as the need for communication bandwidth became more severe [48, 49, 50], and attention returned to optics. A current survey on the field of optical computing can be found in Feitelson's *Optical Computing* [25]. Other works that cover broad aspects of the field can be found in References [3, 6, 35, 51, 106].

There is a great volume of literature on various aspects of optical computing such as optical bistability, optically nonlinear materials, architectures, number systems, methodologies, *etc*. There is far too much work to categorize it all here, so the focus is on projects that have had the greatest influence on the design of general purpose digital optical computers. Except for neural networks, discussion on analog optical computing is intentionally omitted. Error accumulation and accuracy limit the extent analog computing can enjoy in both electronic and optical technologies. There will always be special applications for analog optics such as signal processing, matrix-vector multiplication, and neural networks so the significance of analog optics is not meant to be lessened here, but the role analog optics is likely to play must be placed in perspective with digital optics.

Huang's symbolic substitution [49], which is a parallel method of binary pattern replacement has had a significant influence on the field of optical computing.

Progress has been made in optical implementations [8, 9, 11, 79, 119] and in computing methods [50, 65, 85, 86, 89, 90] based on symbolic substitution. Shadow-casting [116] was introduced at least as early as symbolic substitution in 1983, and offers interesting methods for performing spatial logic. The Digital Optical Cellular Image Processor (DOCIP) approach [56] also enjoys support for its generality and simple hardware requirements. Other work on computing methods [113, 123] for specific applications increased awareness in the diversity of techniques made available through optics. Neural computing has also spurred optical computing research [1, 99] and is currently a rapidly moving area.

There has been progress in guided-wave optics using fibers [107], Ti:LiNbO$_3$ switching elements [46], new approaches using integrated optics [120, 121, 122], and optical interconnects for Very Large Scale Integration (VLSI) [36].

There has been ongoing work in numerical methods using optics such as matrix-vector computing [4, 101], optical linear algebra [13], modified signed digit (MSD) arithmetic [77], number theory [29, 53, 55, 83], and signal processing [24, 59, 74, 103].

The success of digital optics depends heavily on advances in optical hardware, and a number of efforts have focused on device design [30, 31, 32, 63, 68, 75, 76, 82, 111, 120], acoustooptic modulators [37], interconnection networks using fibers [36, 107] and free-space implementations of perfect shuffles [10, 23], crossovers [60], split/shift/combine setups [11, 98, 116], crossbars [61], data manipulators [14] and holographic interconnects [127].

Optical cellular logic has been influenced by the early work of von Neumann [12] on self-reproducing automata and later work by Codd [16] and Langton [72]. Current work on cellular automata that has also influenced optical cellular logic can be found in References [117, 124] and optical versions described in References [21, 56, 126].

Only recently have general purpose digital optical design techniques come about that are tailored for technology available today while providing sufficient extensibility for future systems. The methodology presented in this book provides a foundation for digital design techniques that promote regularity in structure and simplicity in design methods, while providing sufficient extensibility to meet the needs of larger and faster systems.

Chapter 2
Optical Logic Devices and Interconnects

We can dream up all sorts of possibilities for a light-based computer, but it is the physical implementation that lends credibility to our ideas. Significant areas of consideration are the optical logic gates, optical interconnects, and supporting hardware such as light sources, cooling apparatus, mounts, *etc*. This chapter looks into a few of the optical switching devices and optical interconnects that are relevant to the methodology presented in Chapter 4. Supporting hardware is not detailed here because the purpose of this chapter is to introduce enough of the hardware for the reader to identify constraints and considerations in creating architectures without getting bogged down in detail.

2.1 Optical switching devices

A design philosophy based on regularity in structure and simplicity in design methods is supported in this book without making a commitment to a particular optical logic device, although some minimal features are assumed. Characteristics expected of optical logic devices are that they support a fan-in and fan-out of at least two, comprise a logically complete set such as {AND, OR}, {AND}, or {NOR}, support indefinite cascadability, require low switching power, switch at high rates with respect to electronics, and have signal inputs and outputs oriented normal to the surface of the device substrate so that free space is used for interconnection. Devices that meet these goals to some degree include the SEED [76, 82], OLE [63], other etalon type devices making use of multiple quantum wells, and other semiconductor devices [32]. No requirement is made of optical bistability [30] although optical bistability has been a traditional area of research. Other devices have been well-represented in the field such as liquid crystal logic gates [68] and are suitable for the methodology described in Chapter 4 if the high speed goal is relaxed. Only three semiconductor devices are described here in the interest of exposing the reader to a few currently promising devices. Device research and development is a quickly moving area and it would be a distraction to devote much space to it here since the goal of the text is to support a design philosophy that is independent of the device specifics.

2.1.1 Self electro-optic effect devices (SEEDs)

The self electro-optic effect device (SEED) is based on an electrically coupled optical modulator and detector pair. The SEED is made up of approximately 1200 alternating layers of GaAs and GaAlAs in an 8μm thick quantum well structure placed inside a PIN photodiode detector as shown in Figure 2.1.

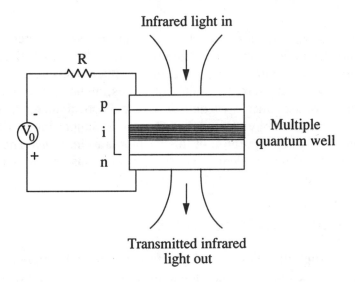

Figure 2.1: *Schematic of the self-electrooptic effect bistable device.*

When light is applied to the detector, a current is generated that reduces the potential across the quantum well. When a strong enough current is created, the positive feedback allows the device to retain its state after the light source is removed. One of the operating modes of the device is to pass light of low intensity and to absorb light at high intensity, implementing negating logic. The electric properties of the device make it easy to work with on an optical bench, and since communication is handled optically, the system speed of a computer made up of these devices is limited only by the device speed. Expected operating rates are several hundred megahertz, although current devices have only been operated at megahertz rates in systems [97]. A fabricated array of SEEDs is shown in Figure 2.2.

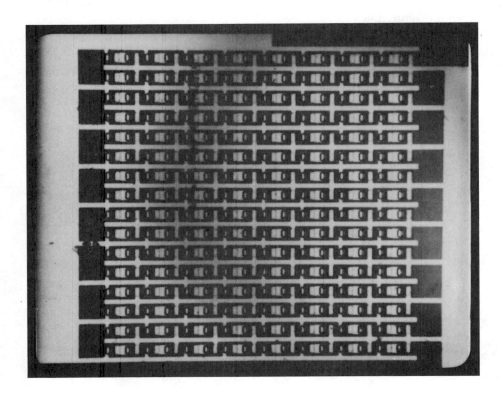

Figure 2.2: *Array of S-SEEDs with a 40μm spacing between device mesas.*

2.1.2 Optical logic etalons (OLEs)

The optical logic etalon (OLE) [63] has potential for being a fast optical logic device if it can be developed for operation in a digital system. A schematic of the OLE is shown in Figure 2.3. An optically nonlinear material such as GaAs/GaAlAs is sandwiched between two mirrors that are spaced an integral number of half wavelengths apart. Two wavelengths are involved, the *pump* wavelength β_0 and the *probe* wavelength β_1. Data is carried by the pump wavelength which interacts with the medium, so that the index of refraction of the material changes for the probe wavelength. The pump beam controls the transmission of the probe beam by tuning the cavity (or detuning the cavity, depending on the mode of operation). The transmitted probe beam then acts as the pump beam for a second stage device that uses β_0 as the probe beam, so that the system can be cascaded. As of this writing, the second stage device has not been developed with sufficient gain to close the system but it is expected that cascadable OLEs will be developed in the near future. A fabricated array of OLEs is shown in Figure 2.4.

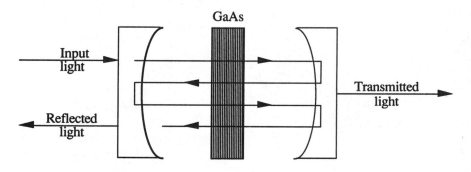

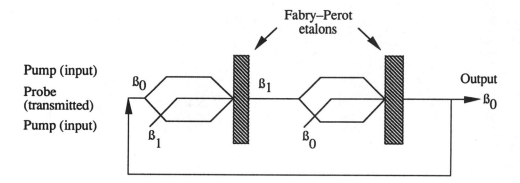

Figure 2.3: *Nonlinear Fabry-Perot etalon (left) and two wavelength operation of OLE nonlinear Fabry-Perot etalons (right).*

Figure 2.4: *Arrays of optical logic etalons (OLEs), also called microresonators. Devices are a few microns in diameter on 4μm centers. Logic gates are etched about 8μm deep. Operating speed is 30ps at room temperature, and the logic operation is two-input, two-output NOR. Inputs enter the tops and output beams emerge on the bottom sides, through the substrate.*

2.1.3 Interference filters

Interference filters [110] are responsible for drawing some early attention to optical computing that spurred a number of device research efforts. Interference filters are comprised of alternating layers of high and low refractive index material such as ZnSe and ThF_4, respectively. Layers are spaced an integral number of quarter wavelengths apart, and two beams interact through the medium by affecting the optically nonlinear ZnSe in the center of the structure which tunes or detunes the cavity depending on the mode of operation, as illustrated in Figure 2.5. Resonance creates a strong output beam and a detuned cavity causes absorption resulting in a weak output beam.

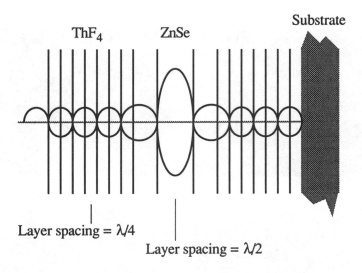

Figure 2.5: *ZnSe interference filter used as a logic device* [110].

The operation of the interference filter as a logic device is based on a relatively slow thermal effect so that the utility of this implementation of the device is limited for competitive systems, but the simplicity of the device fabrication makes it attractive for benchtop experiments.

2.2 Free-space optical interconnects

There is debate over the merits of regular free-space interconnects and irregular[1] free-space interconnects. Irregular free-space interconnects allow for arbitrary point to point communication between logic gates. This makes a mapping from a functional description to a physical implementation easy. A problem with this approach is that optical pulses are typically a few picoseconds in duration and a large enough skew may develop between signals to cause race conditions, and timing simulations will be as necessary as they are now for VLSI. In addition, irregularity in the interconnection medium often results in the input plane being subdivided into a number of pupils, which translates to larger spot sizes in the

---

[1]The degree of regularity is also referred to as the degree of space variance, which describes the local behavior of connections. If the directions of the device output beams are the same for all points on an array, then the interconnect is said to be *space-invariant*.

output plane, forcing a larger spot separation than would otherwise be needed. The result is lower spatial bandwidth (fewer signals in the same area).

Regular free-space interconnects force the mapping from functional description to physical implementation into a predefined layout, which translates to wider and deeper circuits than irregular interconnects would yield. However, signal skews can be kept within femtoseconds, spatial bandwidth is not sacrificed, optical interconnects can be implemented with off-the-shelf glass components, and the circuits are not that much wider or deeper. Thus regular free-space interconnects may be effectively used for interconnecting optical logic gates.

2.2.1 Properties of regular interconnects

Consider a parallel adder circuit that sums eight numbers. A balanced binary tree[1] can be used to add the numbers in the fewest number of levels as shown in Figure 2.6. Addition is an associative operation, which means that the order in which the numbers are added has no influence on the final result.[2] The numbers might just as well have been added in the order shown in Figure 2.7. Normally, a circuit designer will prefer the first adder because the regularity of the interconnects reduces signal skews and makes layouts more manageable. This implies that there is a large amount of freedom given to the architect of an eight-number parallel adder, most of which has no significant influence on the target machine. Since a large amount of freedom available to the hardware designer is unused, we can expect that if we take some of that freedom away, that there will be no great loss in the performance of the target machine. This philosophy is exploited in Chapter 4 where complexity analysis shows that regular interconnects can be used at the gate level without introducing a large cost in circuit depth or breadth.

The remainder of this section provides background on properties of regular interconnects that will be used in later chapters. The section that follows describes optical implementations of these interconnects.

---

[1]A tree is balanced if the number of nodes in each subtree of the root node differ by no more than one and every subtree is balanced.

[2]Actually, the order of addition *does* make a difference in some calculations due to roundoff error. For example, if only five digits of accuracy are allowed for a floating point operation, and if the numbers 1352.8, 2.05, and 2.07 are added from left to right the result will be 1356.8, but if the numbers are added from right to left, the result will be 1356.9.

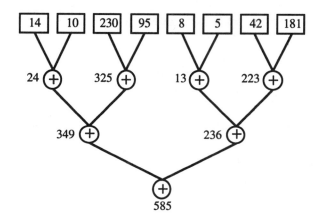

Figure 2.6: *Balanced binary adder tree for summing eight numbers.*

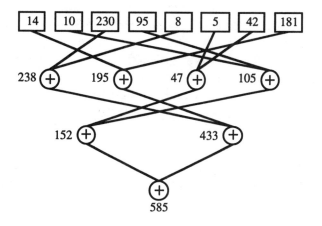

Figure 2.7: *An alternative adder tree.*

For free space optics, $log_2 N$ interconnects [26] are considered for connections between logic gates because fast optical logic devices are limited to small fan-ins and fan-outs [98] such as two. The class of $O(log N)$ networks[1] is favored because those networks allow an arbitrary connection to be made in the fewest

---

[1]The construct $O(log N)$ is read "of the class order $log N$", and labels networks that grow logarithmically along some parameter such as space or time as N (the number of inputs, for example) grows linearly.

number of levels. To see why this is the case, consider the $O(N)$ mesh interconnect shown in Figure 2.8. In order to connect any two of the N elements in a row, at most $\lfloor N/2 \rfloor$ time steps are needed. For large networks this communication cost is too expensive when compared to an $O(log\ N)$ network such as the *banyan* shown in Figure 2.9. If a binary address is assigned to each column of the banyan network as shown and the logical exclusive-OR (XOR) is taken between the addresses of any two columns, then the set bits in the XOR pattern indicate on what levels the angled paths are taken to route a signal from one column to another. For example, in order to set up a path from column 011 to column 101, the pattern XOR (011, 101) = 110 specifies that the angled path should be taken at the first level, the angled path at the second level, and the straight path at the last level as shown in the highlighted connections of Figure 2.9. For an N-wide network, $\lceil log_2 N \rceil$ bits are needed to represent the address so $\lceil log_2 N \rceil$ levels are needed to connect any two elements in the worst case.

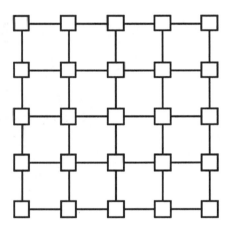

Figure 2.8: *Two-dimensional nearest-neighbor mesh interconnect.*

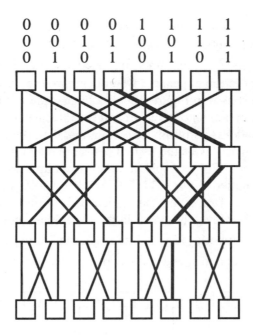

Figure 2.9: *Banyan interconnect with path 011 → 111 → 101 → 101 highlighted.*

At any level in the banyan network, only three angles of connections are needed. Each level is made up of *butterfly* interconnects such as the one shown in Figure 2.10. A butterfly on a string of length $N = 2^n$ can be described as an exchange of the least significant bit (LSB) and most significant bit (MSB) (bit 0 and bit $n - 1$) in the binary address x of each element a_x of the string:

$$a_x \rightarrow a_{Exchange(x)}$$

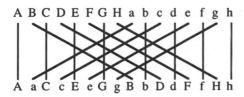

Figure 2.10: *16-wide butterfly.*

The three angles of connections in the butterfly are a copy operation (for all elements of the string having a binary address with LSB = MSB), a shift to the right by $N/2 - 1$ (for all elements of the string having a binary address with LSB $= 1$ and MSB $= 0$) and a shift to the left by $N/2 - 1$ (for the rest of the elements).

A variation of this network produces a *data manipulator network* shown in Figure 2.11 [14]. The data manipulator network shown here differs from the conventional data manipulator because wraparound at the edges is not allowed, owing to the difficulty in performing optical wraparound. The interconnection pattern of the data manipulator without wraparound is expressed by:

$$a_x \rightarrow \text{mod}\,(B, a + N/2)$$

and

$$a_x \rightarrow \text{mod}\,(B, a - N/2)$$

where B is the width of the butterflies used in a particular stage, N is the width of the network, and *mod* is the modulo function.

Figure 2.11: *Data manipulator network without wraparound.*

The *crossover* interconnect [60] can be described by the permutations:

$$a_x \rightarrow a_x$$

and

$$a_x \rightarrow \text{Gray}\,(C, a - N/2)$$

where C is the width of crossovers used in a particular stage, N is the width of the network, and Gray is a Gray code mapping [15]. The connection patterns achieved with the crossover and the full crossover are shown in Figures 2.12 and 2.13, respectively. The full crossover replaces the $a_x \rightarrow a_x$ straight-through mapping with a Gray code mapping with C replaced by $C/2$.

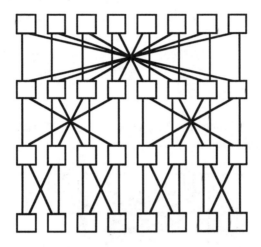

Figure 2.12: *The crossover interconnect.*

Figure 2.13: *The full crossover interconnect.*

The perfect shuffle [114] is a special permutation of the string $(a_0, ..., a_{N-1})$ of length $N = 2^n$. The shuffle can be expressed as a cyclic left rotation (ROL) of the binary addresses of the elements:

$$a_x \rightarrow a_{ROL(x)}$$

Figure 2.14 illustrates two forms of a one-dimensional perfect shuffle interconnect for $N = 16$, and a network made up of these shuffles is shown in Figure 2.15. The perfect shuffle is commonly used for interconnecting array processors [73, 108], permutation networks [71, 93, 125], sorting [70], and for special algorithms such as the fast Fourier transformation (FFT) [17] and Hadamard transformation [59].

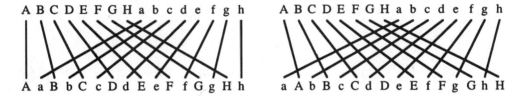

Figure 2.14: *16-wide one-dimensional perfect shuffles. The right hand shuffle is obtained by shifting the upper case outputs of the left hand shuffle to the right by two places.*

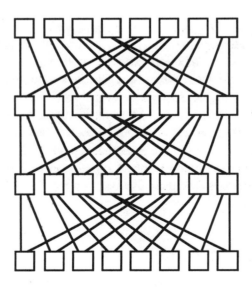

Figure 2.15: *Perfect shuffle connected network.*

The perfect shuffle, banyan, and crossover networks can be mapped among each other as shown in Figure 2.16 because they share a property called *isomorphism*. One network can be mapped onto another by replacing corresponding connection patterns and relabeling nodes. The operations inside of the nodes remain unchanged. For the discussion here, the nodes represent two-input, two-output logic gates.

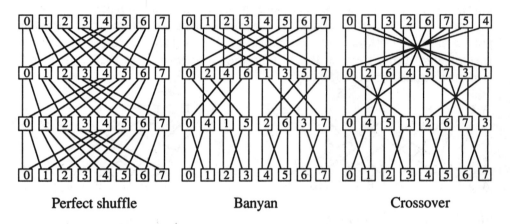

| Perfect shuffle | Banyan | Crossover |

Figure 2.16: *Isomorphism among perfect shuffle, banyan, and crossover interconnects.*

2.2.2 Holographic irregular interconnects
Computer generated holograms (CGHs) can be made to implement a wide range of regular and irregular connection patterns. In theory, any lens system can be collapsed into a single lens, which can be created through holography. A hologram can image a source, such as the output from an optical logic gate, onto a number of different output points. An array of subholograms can image many sources onto many different sets of output points as illustrated in Figure 2.17. As mentioned earlier in this chapter, the price that is paid for this flexibility is reduced spatial bandwidth and the introduction of signal skews. Losses and wavelength sensitivity are other issues that must also be considered.

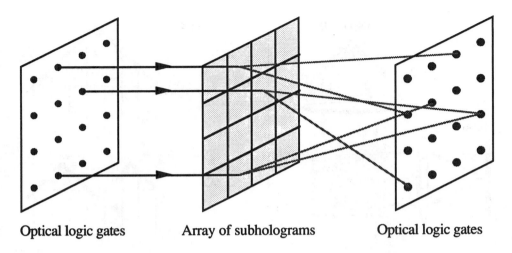

Optical logic gates   Array of subholograms   Optical logic gates

Figure 2.17: *An array of subholograms images the outputs of an array of optical logic gates onto the inputs of another array of optical logic gates.*

2.2.3 Optical implementation of the crossover

An optical implementation of the crossover networks can be realized efficiently with a simple setup that uses prism arrays of varying periods. Figure 2.18 shows an optical design of one stage of the crossover network and an optical implementation is shown in Figure 2.19. An input image is split into two identical images. One image is reflected by a mirror to the output plane. The other image is permuted according to the period of the prism array and is combined with the reflected image onto the output plane. For a full crossover, the mirror is replaced with a prism array of half the period of the other prism array.

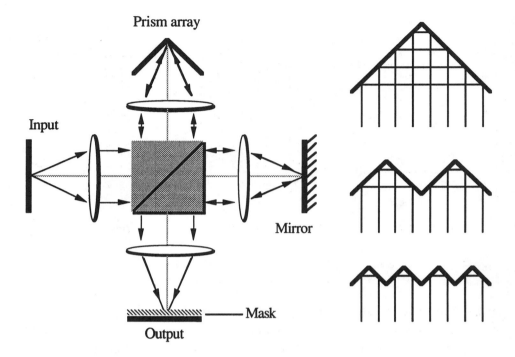

Figure 2.18: *Optical crossover interconnect. A two-dimensional array of input beams is split into two identical copies. One copy is imaged onto a mirror and is reflected back through the system to the output, while the other copy is imaged onto a prism array that permutes the beams according to the period of the prism array. Combined arrays are slightly displaced in the output plane so that a single mask serves both images. Connections achieved with different prism array periods are shown in the right panel.*

Although this implementation of the crossover does not throw away light except for losses in the components, the optical distance through the system may be several hundred picoseconds. For subnanosecond switching speeds this latency cannot be tolerated except for a few high throughput applications like signal processing, packet switching, and matrix operations that can take advantage of gate-level pipelining.

Figure 2.19: *Optical implementation of the crossover interconnect. The prism array is held in the mount closest to the reader and the mirror is held in the mount opposite the camera. The beam-splitter is a cube of glass in the center of the structure, between the camera and the mirror. The input image enters the system on the far side of the optical bench opposite the prism array, and the camera captures the output image. (Photograph provided by the courtesy of Jürgen Jahns, AT&T Bell Laboratories.)*

2.2.4 Optical implementation of the perfect shuffle

A horizontal perfect shuffle is performed on a two dimensional array by splitting the input image into two identical images, magnifying each image by two, interlacing the images, and isolating the middle portion as shown in Figure 2.20 [10]. This particular implementation of the perfect shuffle includes a magnification step which may be a problem for small devices, with diameters near the diffraction limit (on the order of a micron for wavelengths near 850nm).

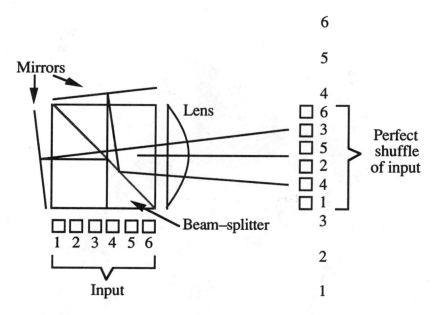

Figure 2.20: *Optical implementation of the perfect shuffle.*

The advantage of the shuffle-type interconnects over the others is that the interconnection pattern is identical for interconnecting every stage of logic gates. This means that only one optical setup is needed instead of $\log_2 N$ different setups as for the crossover network. A major disadvantage of the perfect shuffle is that the best known techniques for implementing optical perfect shuffles discard light by only using the center section of the output plane or involve magnification or complex grating structures which introduce difficulty for devices with dimensions near the diffraction limit.

2.2.5 Microoptics and the split+shift

The distances between device arrays can be reduced if the glass components are fabricated as thin as possible and the array dimensions are reduced. For example, a 32 x 32 array of devices spaced 2μm apart between device centers can be interconnected with flat optics in just a few millimeters, so that a 10ps cycle time can be achieved before the array-to-array distances again become significant. From an engineering standpoint, smaller array sizes are preferable because lens aberrations are reduced and manufacturability is improved. Bandwidth to and from the arrays is not limited by pin count as it is for conventional VLSI so that the architectural implications of moving from a few dense chips to many sparse chips are minimized. A few characteristics of scaling down to microoptics are summarized in Figure 2.21 [62]:

Devices per array	$N^2 \rightarrow N^2/s^2$
Number of arrays	$M \rightarrow s^2M$
Power per array	$P \rightarrow P/s^2$
Intensity	$I \rightarrow I$
Lens diameter	$D \rightarrow D/s$
Lens aberrations	$A \rightarrow A/s$
Latency	$\tau \rightarrow\ < \tau/s$
Temperature rise	$\Delta T \rightarrow \Delta T/s$

Figure 2.21: *The effects of scaling a system down by a scaling factor* s *to microoptic sizes are summarized [62].*

As shown in the table, significant aspects of system behavior that are affected by a microoptics approach are lower operating temperatures, smaller lens aberrations, and smaller gate-to-gate latencies. A conceptualization of part of a microoptic system is shown in Figure 2.22.

Fewer optical components are involved for this approach which improves manufacturability but reduces interconnection flexibility, which translates to wider and deeper circuits. The cost of the larger circuits is small when compared to the gains in manufacturability summarized in Figure 2.21. The reduced flexibility comes about because there is not enough room in a few millimeters to split an image into two copies and separately permute each image before recombining as can be done for the other interconnects. Magnification is not allowed because device diameters are near the diffraction limit and tight focusing must be maintained. The interconnection patterns result from simple split+shift operations, where the shift from one stage to the next varies by only small numbers such as 16 or less. An example of a split+shift connection pattern achievable in a microoptic setup is shown in Figure 2.23 for three stages.

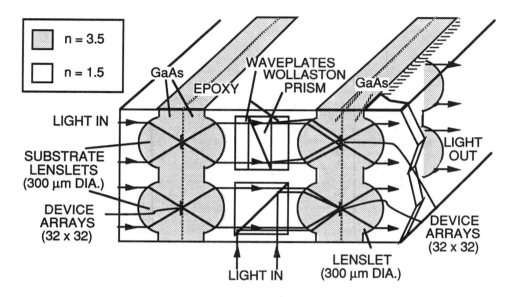

Figure 2.22: *Conceptualization of a microoptic system. Arrays of optical logic gates are placed between fabricated lenses that image optical signals onto the next device arrays. Prisms and beam-splitters are used for interconnection and bringing in optical power. The system is made rigid with epoxy. (Illustration provided by the courtesy of Jack Jewell, AT&T Bell Laboratories.)*

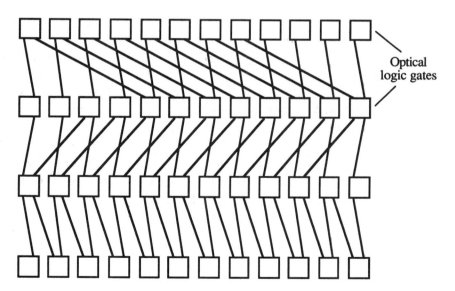

Figure 2.23: *Connection pattern for three optical logic stages of a split+shift setup.*

Chapter 3
A Few Architectural Approaches for General Purpose Optical Computing

There is one major approach supported in this text for designing circuits for a digital optical computer, described in the last section of this chapter and throughout Chapter 4. There are other approaches, and six of them are described in this chapter that have enjoyed visibility. A number of approaches have been left out because the goal here is not to provide a general survey but to give the reader enough background to appreciate the significance of the Chapter 4 approach, in maintaining regularity in the hardware and simplicity in the design methods.

There is some orthogonality to the approaches described in this chapter that include: (1) digital all-optical with free space interconnects, (2) hybrid optical / electronic, (3) analog optical, and (4) guided wave interconnected optical logic. Within the digital all-optical approaches, regular free-space interconnects support a strong trend in digital optics toward manufacturability. Uniform devices arrays, simple optics with few components, scalability to large systems, and methods for dealing with faults are emphasized in the regular free-space approach .

3.1 Symbolic substitution

An influential work in digital optical computing is Huang's *symbolic substitution* [49], which is a method of computing based on binary pattern substitution. The general idea is to search for a two-dimensional pattern in a binary grid and to replace that pattern with another pattern everywhere the search pattern is found.

An example is shown in Figure 3.1. The search pattern is called the *left hand side* (LHS) of the transformation rule and the pattern that replaces the LHS is called the *right hand side* (RHS) of the transformation rule. In Figure 3.1, the LHS of the rule is satisfied at two locations, so the RHS is written at those locations. Any cells that do not contribute to the LHS pattern disappear after the rule is applied. A number of rules can be applied in series or in parallel for an indefinite number of iterations to realize complex functions. Transformation rules can be customized to perform specific functions such as addition (described in this section) or they may be made to perform more general functions such as Boolean logic primitives in which case the configuration of the grid can be customized to implement specific functions [86].

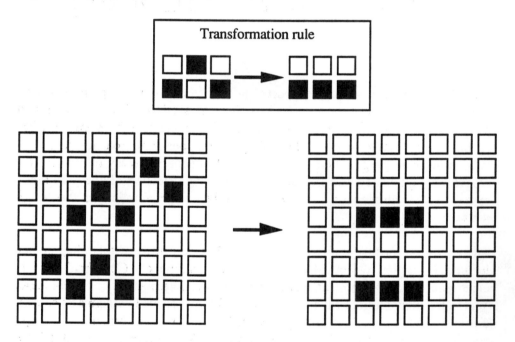

Figure 3.1: *Symbolic substitution. Transformation rule (top), initial grid (bottom left), and transformed grid after applying the transformation rule (bottom right).*

A schematic diagram of an optical setup for a single transformation rule with four cells in the LHS and four cells in the RHS is shown in Figure 3.2. A two-dimensional input pattern is combined with a two-dimensional control image produced by imaging light through a mask onto optically nonlinear OR array A. The feedback path from array A is split into four identical copies which are shifted and superimposed onto AND array B to implement the LHS of the rule. Array B performs a threshold operation and normalizes the signals. The output of array B is split into four copies which are shifted and superimposed onto array A to implement the RHS of the rule, normalize signals, and provide an output. Figure 3.3 shows a time sequence of symbolic substitution using this setup. In this example, the input image (A) contains one binary pattern that matches the LHS of the rule. The input image is split into four identical copies (B), which are each shifted (C) and superimposed (D) according to the positions of the bits in the LHS of the rule. Each of the bits in the LHS is one position away from the center cell in the *x* and *y* directions, so each image is shifted according to its distance from the center cell. A threshold operation (E) sets all cells to 0 except those cells that have the original intensity after the images are superimposed. The array (F) is then split into four identical images (G) which are shifted (H) and superimposed (I) according to the RHS pattern. The intensity values in the final image are restored by regeneration element B (J).

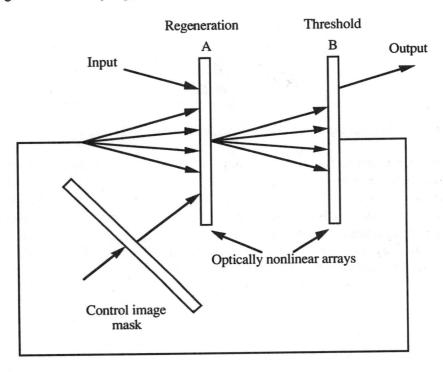

Figure 3.2: *Schematic of optical implementation of symbolic substitution. Optically nonlinear arrays are connected with space-invariant imaging operations. Beam-splitters or spatial filtering is used to split and recombine the images. A fixed control mask provides a customizing pattern that provides a means for programming the system.*

A   B   C   D E F   G   H   I J K

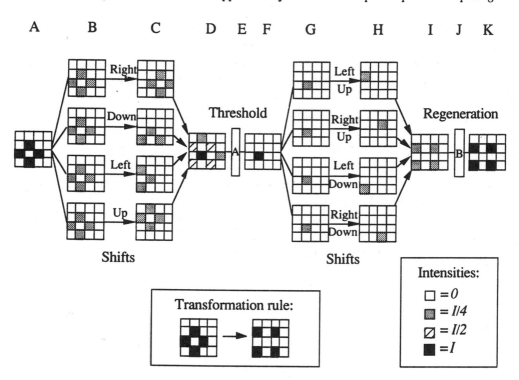

Figure 3.3: *Time sequence of symbolic substitution for a 4x4 system.*

When more than one rule is applied in parallel, an implementation reported in Reference [11] can be used. A setup for implementing four rules with two cells in the LHS and RHS of each rule is shown in Figure 3.4. The input image is passed through a cascade of beam-splitters to produce four copies. Each copy is passed to a pattern recognizer/pattern substituter pair and the signals are regenerated by an array of optically nonlinear logic gates. The outputs are combined on the output plane through a cascade of beam-combiners. The system can be fed back onto itself for an indefinite number of cycles.

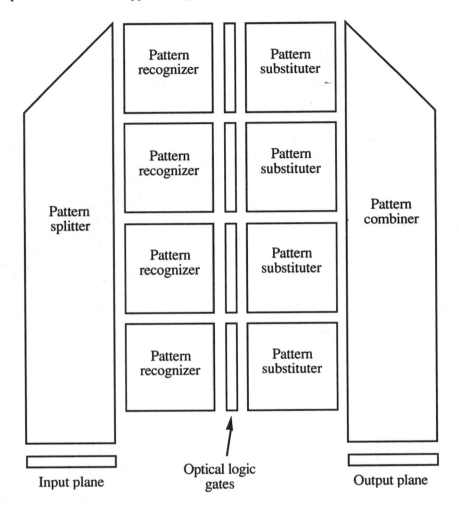

Figure 3.4: *Optical implementation of four 2x2 symbolic substitution rules. The input image is split into four copies that are each passed to a pattern recognizer/pattern substituter pair. The outputs from the pattern substituters are combined onto the output plane.*

The pattern recognizers and pattern substituters can be implemented with Michelson interferometers (Figure 3.5) as reported in Reference [11]. The tilts of the mirrors correspond to two cell positions in the LHS or RHS of a rule. The interferometer performs the split, shift, and combine operations. The binary adder described in the next few paragraphs uses four rules with two cells on the LHS and RHS, so the multi-rule system described here maps well for addition.

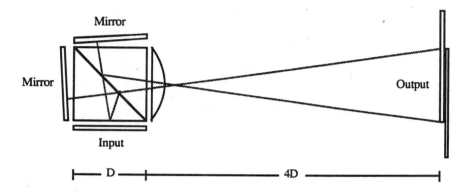

Figure 3.5: *Michelson interferometer implementation of split/shift/combine operation.*

A method of binary addition based on symbolic substitution is introduced in Reference [49]. The method emulates binary addition as a human would normally perform addition by hand, by assigning a transformation rule to each of the operations involved in adding two binary digits as shown below:

$$0 + 0 = 0 \qquad \text{carry} = 0$$
$$0 + 1 = 1 \qquad \text{carry} = 0$$
$$1 + 0 = 1 \qquad \text{carry} = 0$$
$$1 + 1 = 0 \qquad \text{carry} = 1$$

Binary numbers can be represented in the dual-rail logic system where each binary digit is represented as a pair that has one bit on and one bit off. The spatial location of the bit that is on determines the state of the pair. For example, binary 0 can be represented as 01 and binary 1 can be represented as 10. The binary number 010 would then be represented as 011001. A logical negation is made by swapping bits within a pair.

Figure 3.6 shows four rules proposed by Huang [49] that implement binary addition in dual-rail logic. The rules correspond to each of the dual-rail operations:

$$01 + 01 = 01 \qquad \text{carry} = 01$$
$$01 + 10 = 10 \qquad \text{carry} = 01$$
$$10 + 01 = 10 \qquad \text{carry} = 01$$
$$10 + 10 = 01 \qquad \text{carry} = 10$$

Dark cells are fixed to the *on* state via the mask shown in the block diagram of Figure 3.2. These four rules are all that are needed to add two indefinitely long binary strings.

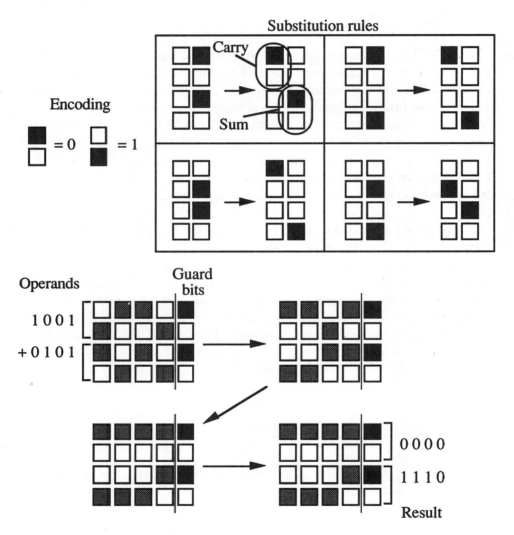

Figure 3.6: *Binary addition via symbolic substitution.*

More complex operations such as multiplication, division, and matrix multiplication are described in Reference [85] with unrestricted freedom given in the number and size of transformation rules. The mechanism that implements the rules is more complex because it must be capable of shifting arbitrary distances in unit time, and no restrictions are made on fan-in and fan-out which makes that approach less practical.

3.2 The QWEST model

The QWEST model makes use of a device that is based on the Quantum Well Envelope State Transition effect. The effect operates within the conduction band rather than between conduction and valence bands, so a logic gate based on this effect can be faster and less sensitive to temperature fluctuations than devices based on band-to-band transitions like the SEED and OLE. The basic model is an entire computer made up of a solid cube of optical logic gates and waveguide connections in a three-dimensional stack as shown in Figure 3.7. Because of the QWEST's relative insensitivity to temperature variation, the machine can develop temperatures up to 300°C before there is a need for special cooling.

The philosophy behind the approach is that there is no need to redesign the computer designer. Optical logic gates are oriented parallel to the substrate and connections are made through waveguides on layers and through grating couplers between layers. The model is similar to conventional VLSI except that three-dimensional structures are more easily fabricated since layer to layer interfaces are performed optically. The approach has tremendous potential but also has considerable risk because it relies on advanced fabrication that is not sufficiently developed.

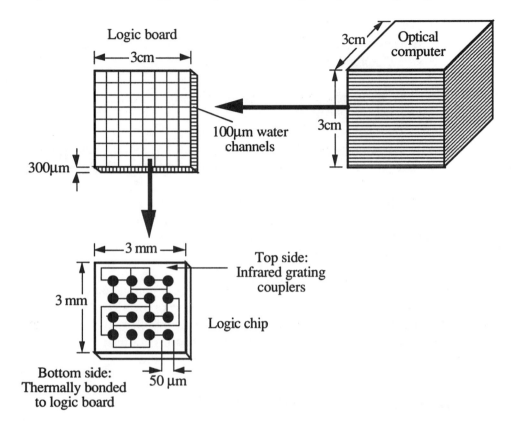

Figure 3.7: *Conceptualization of the QWEST based model of a digital computer. The entire computer fits inside a 3cm cube and is comprised of stacks of optically interconnected boards made up of optical logic chips. Waveguides connect optical logic devices on the chips and grating couplers are used for coupling optical power into the waveguides.*

3.3 Neural computing

Neural computing has enjoyed a fair amount of attention in recent years. Some neural networks are capable of general purpose computing so a short discussion is included here for that reason. Three common features among neural network models that interest the optical computing community include [5]:

> (1) A large number of simple processing elements (PE's) are arranged in densely connected layers.

(2) Interconnections among PE's have analog weights indicating the strength of the interconnections.

(3) The interconnection weights evolve under the influence of external weights.

Photorefractive crystals record connection images in real time (on the order of video rates) and provide one method for implementing changeable connection weights. Since the dense connectivity is the most significant architectural limitation of neural networks, it makes sense to look into optics for a solution. The PE's can be implemented with conventional electronics that perform the simple functions of summation and thresholding at the response rate of the connection medium.

The goal of this chapter is to broaden the reader's view of general purpose *digital* optical computing models, but analog neural networks are mentioned because of their high visibility and potential for general purpose computing, even though the technology is primarily analog. Speed and generality are significant problems, so the use of optical neural networks is not explored further here.

3.4 Optical interconnects for VLSI

One of the most severe speed limitations in electronic digital circuits is caused by the energy required to drive a signal off of a chip. It is suggested here that on-chip communication should be handled electrically, and that chip-to-chip communication should be handled optically. An interconnection scheme based on this idea [36] is shown in Figure 3.8.

In Figure 3.8, a hologram images light sources onto optoelectronic detectors using free space as the interconnection medium. One possible device for this approach is the Si/PLZT [75] which can be fabricated with existing Si technology. This approach makes sense for the near term because it removes the most severe bottleneck for current VLSI without radically changing fabrication technology, although some new complexity is added in assembly and at some point this approach may no longer pay off due to signal skews, routing latency, and power requirements.

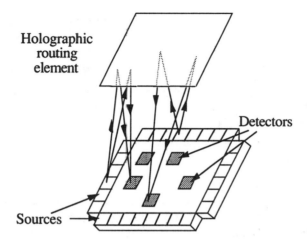

Figure 3.8: *Optical sources and detectors are connected with a holographic routing element. Optical interconnects can be used between sections on a chip and between chips without introducing power and signal skew problems associated with driving electrical lines off of a chip* [36].

3.5 A bit-serial optical computer

An optical serial computer [67] has been proposed and partially built as of this writing. The system makes use of less than 100 lithium niobate couplers, with the electrical input replaced by an optoelectronic detector as shown in Figure 3.9. The goal of the approach is to create a general purpose all-optical digital computer with a small number of switching components. Spools of fiber implement a delay line memory and the 55-100 logic gates implement a small arithmetic logic unit (ALU) that operates on the memory. The lithium niobate switches can pass signals on the order of several gigahertz, but the control input that sets the two channel switch in bypass or cross mode has a smaller bandwidth, on the order of megahertz. An application that exploits this speed disparity is high bandwidth telephone switching, where channels are opened and closed infrequently with respect to the bit rate.

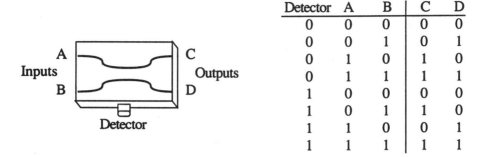

Detector	A	B	C	D
0	0	0	0	0
0	0	1	0	1
0	1	0	1	0
0	1	1	1	1
1	0	0	0	0
1	0	1	1	0
1	1	0	0	1
1	1	1	1	1

Figure 3.9: *Lithium niobate switch with an optoelectronic detector at the control input. A and B are routed to C and D respectively, or are cross coupled to opposite outputs as shown in the function table, depending on the state of the control input.*

3.6 Acoustooptic modulator based logic

Acoustooptic modulators are electrically controlled devices that change the angle of deflection of a beam of light via a pressure wave sent through the device. An architecture based on this concept [38] uses electrical logic signals to drive what is effectively a matrix of acoustooptic modulators, that are imaged onto a second modulator matrix that makes use of electrical control signals to enable or disable the original signals. This is effectively a multiple input AND function. The result is then imaged onto a single OR device that only needs to detect the presence or absence of light.

Although the AND-OR operation is very simple, the technique can be applied iteratively to realize complex functions. Expected operating rates are on the order of 200 MHz, which situates this technology somewhere between conventional VLSI and the expected operating rates of systems based on quantum well devices. There are problems with extending the technique to large systems because lossless beam combination for the OR stage is difficult and consumes a significant amount of optical power.

3.7 Free-space regular interconnects

Finally, an approach making use of regular free-space interconnects is described here because of the emphasis on regularity in structure and simplicity in design methods. This approach is based on the idea of regular arrays of identical optical logic devices interconnected in free space with a regular structure such as an optical crossover network. A conceptual layout of an optical computer based on arrays of optical logic devices and crossover interconnects is shown in Figure 3.10. Optical signals travel orthogonal to the device substrates, through alternating crossover stages and logic stages. The system is fed back onto itself and an input channel and an output channel are provided allowing for a conventional model of a digital circuit. Feedback is imaged with a single row vertical shift so that data spirals through the system, allowing a different section of each mask to be used on each pass. This architecture lends itself to an efficient optical implementation [18] which motivates the development of digital design techniques based on this model.

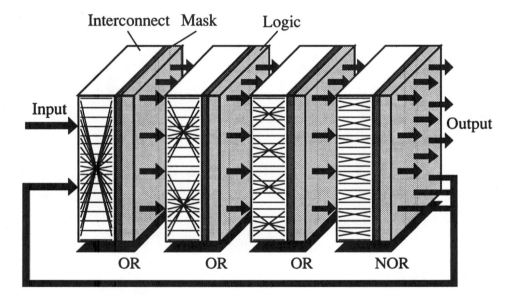

Figure 3.10: *Arrays of optical logic gates are interconnected with crossovers.*

The object of digital design for this model is to map the functional description of a digital circuit onto the regular structure. The positions of the logic gates are fixed, all gates have fan-in and fan-out of two, all devices on the same array perform the same function such as OR or NOR, and the interconnects between arrays are crossovers. The only choices the circuit designer has are the positions of the inputs, the positions of the outputs, and the configurations of the masks that block unwanted connections. A collection of design techniques described in the next chapter aids a computer designer in mapping functions onto this architecture. Claims are supported that hardware complexity as measured in terms of circuit breadth and circuit depth are comparable to other means of interconnection, and that the optics is simpler as a result of the regularity. This approach is described in detail in the next chapter.

Chapter 4
A Methodology for Designing Digital Optical Computers

In this chapter an approach to designing digital optical computers is described for arrays of optical logic gates interconnected in free space. The methodology supports regularity in design and simplicity in the design process. In the sections that follow, regular interconnection schemes are presented for implementing arbitrary functions and memory. The approach is to implement AND-OR logic in an algorithmic manner with predefined connection patterns. Rather than placing connections only where they are needed, a regular connection pattern is put in place in advance of the design and the algorithms show where to remove connections that are *not* needed.

4.1 A design technique based on programmable logic arrays (PLAs)

A *programmable logic array* (PLA) is a topologically regular structure for implementing arbitrary logic functions. A schematic diagram of a four input, four output PLA is shown in Figure 4.1. Four binary inputs i_0, i_1, i_2, i_3 and their complements are arranged in columns on the left side of the PLA. For four binary variables, there are $2^4 = 16$ combinations involving all four variables or their complements, so the inputs to 16 AND gates intersect the inputs for this example. At each crosspoint a programmable fuse (for an electronic PLA) can be enabled or disabled so that a variable or its complement can be included or excluded in the combination as appropriate. The AND matrix is followed by a programmable OR matrix where ANDed combinations are logically ORed to form AND-OR Boolean functions. The PLA is a general component that allows any function or group of functions to be implemented in a regular structure.

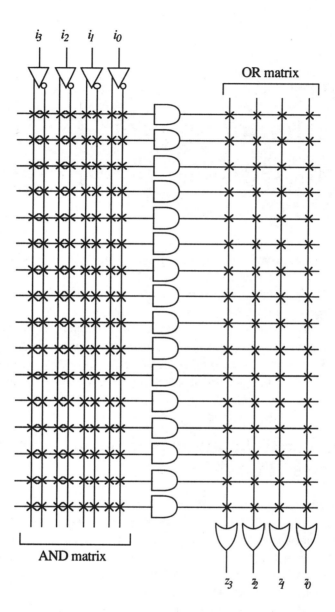

Figure 4.1: *Four function programmable logic array of four variables.*

Optically, the AND and OR gates can be implemented with a uniform array of two input, two output optical AND and OR gates, the fuses can be implemented with two-dimensional masks, and the connections can be provided by an $O(\log N)$ optical interconnect.

The general approach is to first generate all possible unminimized minterms, and then to select and combine the minterms that are needed to implement the functions. This technique is similar to the way functions are generated with electronic PLA's. Normally, both the AND matrix and the OR matrix are programmable. That is the case here as well, but for this section only the programming of the OR matrix is discussed in the interest of keeping the algorithm simple.

Two copies of all 2^m unminimized minterms of m variables are generated in $m + 1$ levels, and the minterms are combined into arbitrary functions in another $m + 1$ levels, giving a maximum depth of $2(m + 1)$ levels to implement any function of m variables. The depth is near-optimal for the worst case (optimal depth for generating any minterm of m variables is $m + 1$ for AND gates with fan-in and fan-out of two and the depth of the OR stage varies with the function being implemented) but gate count is generally higher than when an arbitrary interconnect is used.

4.1.1 The model

The model is made up of customizable regular interconnects and arrays of optically nonlinear logic gates arranged in an AND stage and an OR stage similar to the model described in the last chapter, as shown in Figure 4.2. An array of input beams passes through four banyan connected AND stages and four banyan connected OR stages. Each image is permuted optically in the x dimension and is passed through a mask before being combined onto an array of logic gates. The output is produced in the last OR stage. Feedback paths are imaged back onto the system with a vertical shift so that each row is imaged onto a different part of the masks on each iteration. Although the model is described in terms of banyan interconnects for the sake of clarity in the algorithm to be described, any topologically equivalent interconnect will suffice, such as the perfect shuffle or crossover.

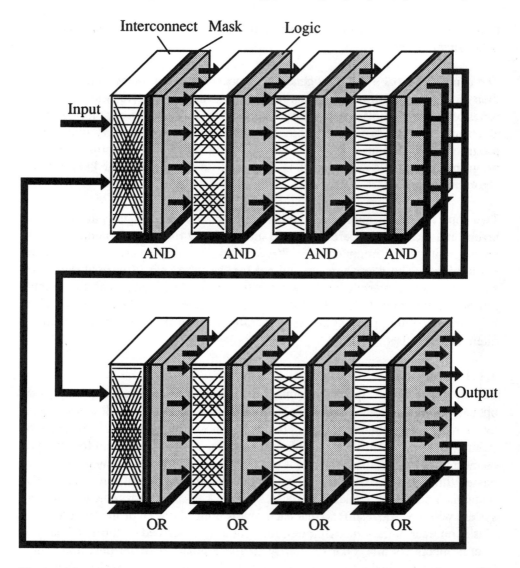

Figure 4.2: *An array of optical signals passes through alternating stages of logic and banyan interconnects. An array of outputs is produced in the last OR stage and feedback to the first AND stage is provided allowing for cascadability. Interconnects are customized with masks that block light at selected locations.*

4.1.2 Generating minterms in the AND stage

A recursive formulation for implementing all unminimized minterms of any number of variables is described in this section. For a network with $m = 1$, the connection pattern shown in Figure 4.3 is used. Unused paths that are masked out are marked with dimmed lines. AND gates with a single input behave as single input AND gates. That is, the output of the gate takes on the same value as the input. This assumption is made only for the purpose of defining the algorithm. The physical implementation can avoid this complexity by using OR-NOR logic as described later in this discussion. Networks for generating minterms of $m > 1$ variables are constructed recursively. For a network with $m = n$, two $n - 1$ networks are placed side by side. A $2^m + 1$ butterfly is added to the top and the $m'th$ variable and its complement are added to the $2^m - 2$ and $2^m - 1$ positions respectively (counting from the left, starting with 0). Connections are added in the top level and the next level to introduce the uncomplemented variable into every minterm on the left and the complemented variable into every minterm on the right. At the top level, the uncomplemented variable is passed to the left $n - 1$ network and the complemented variable is passed to the right $n - 1$ network. At the next level, the uncomplemented variable is connected to the most recently added uncomplemented variable. The complemented variable is connected to the most recently added complemented variable. Finally, the remaining variables are simply passed through to both sides of the network. No other connections are needed.

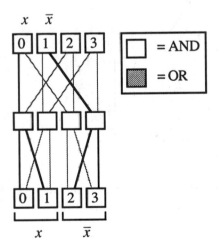

Figure 4.3: *Network for generating minterms of one variable. Flow of information is from the top to the bottom. Unused paths that are masked out are marked with dimmed lines. AND gates with a single input behave as single input AND gates. That is, the output of the gate takes on the same value as the input.*

Example:

To create a network with $m = 2$, place two $m = 1$ networks side by side and add a butterfly of width 2^{m+1} to the top as shown in Figure 4.4. Add the *m'th* variable and its complement to the top row in positions $2^m - 2 = 2$ and $2^m - 1 = 3$ as shown. Connections are made in the top two levels of the network so that the new variable or its complement appears in every minterm. The other input variables are passed from the top stage through to both sides of the network. An $m = 3$ network can be constructed from two $m = 2$ networks as shown in Figure 4.5.

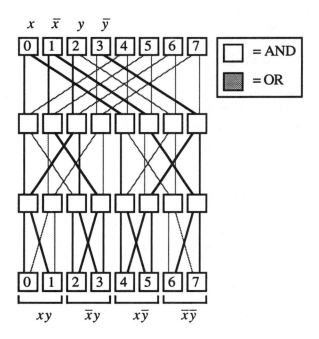

Figure 4.4: *Network for generating minterms of two variables.*

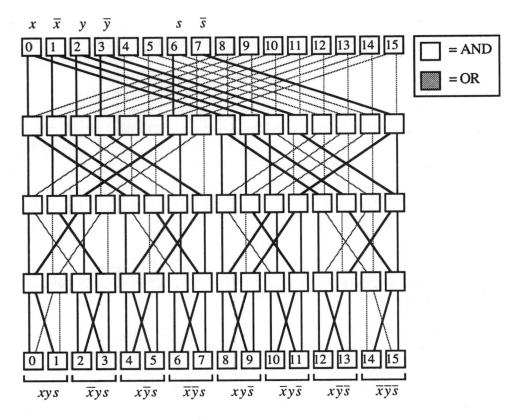

Figure 4.5: *Generation of all three-variable unminimized minterms with a banyan interconnect and two-input, two-output AND gates. Inputs are provided at the top and two outputs for each minterm are produced at the bottom.*

For a network with m input variables and the m corresponding complements the network will be 2^{m+1} gates wide and $m + 1$ levels deep. In Figure 4.5, the input variables are x, y, and s and the complements are $\bar{x}$, $\bar{y}$, and $\bar{s}$. $m = 3$ so the network is $2^{3+1} = 16$ gates wide and $3 + 1 = 4$ levels deep. The eight unminimized minterms are shown at the bottom of the figure.

4.1.3 Generating functions in the OR stage

For a network of width N and logic gates with fan-in and fan-out of two, a path can always be made from any input to any output in $\log_2 N$ levels. The process of generating a path can be viewed as a traversal through a binary tree, whose root is the desired input and whose leaves are the outputs. Each gate is assigned a binary address from 0 to $N - 1$ according to its position from the left. The logical XOR is taken between each input address and the output address. In order to make connections between inputs and outputs, the ith bit is observed on the ith level. If the ith bit is 0, then the straight path is taken, otherwise the angled path is taken. In order to combine minterms to create a function, a separate path is found from each of the needed minterms to the selected output. The paths are then combined to realize the function. Any combination of terms can always be made for both the left subtree and the right subtree. If we are willing to give up the freedom of placing the outputs anywhere we want, then we can get any four combinations of the terms by placing outputs at locations 3, 4, 11, and 12 as shown in Figure 4.7 for a dual-rail serial adder described by the equations shown below:

$$s_{t+1} = \bar{x}y\,s_t + x\bar{y}\,s_t + xy\,\bar{s}_t + xy\,s_t$$
$$\bar{s}_{t+1} = \bar{x}\bar{y}\,\bar{s}_t + \bar{x}y\,s_t + \bar{x}y\,\bar{s}_t + x\bar{y}\,\bar{s}_t$$
$$z_{t+1} = \bar{x}\bar{y}\,s_t + \bar{x}y\,\bar{s}_t + x\bar{y}\,\bar{s}_t + xy\,s_t$$
$$\bar{z}_{t+1} = \bar{x}\bar{y}\,\bar{s}_t + \bar{x}y\,s_t + xy\,\bar{s}_t + x\bar{y}\,s_t$$

In general, however, the positioning of the outputs is determined by the function being implemented.

The minterm generation stage is the same for any function of the same number of variables. This means that the AND stage will be identical for a serial adder, a serial subtractor, a three-bit address decoder, and any other function of three variables. In many cases however, the circuit is wider than it needs to be since unnecessary terms are often generated. This cost is discussed in the next section.

Although the layout algorithm is described in terms of banyan interconnects, a mapping to perfect shuffle or crossover interconnects is straightforward as pointed out in Section 2.2.1. AND and OR logic can also be mapped to OR and NOR logic in a one-to-one manner to match the expected operating modes of optical logic gates. Figures 4.5 and 4.6 have been redrawn with crossovers and OR-NOR logic in Figures 4.8 and 4.9 to illustrate this point. The change of interconnect from banyan to crossover is made independently of the change in logic from AND-OR to OR-NOR. That is, a change in one does not affect the other.

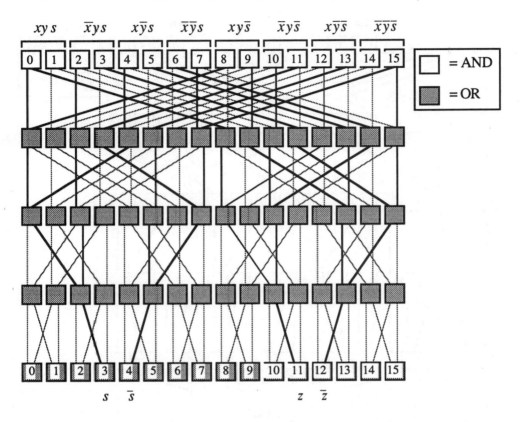

Figure 4.6: *Mapping minterms to state and output functions for a serial adder.*

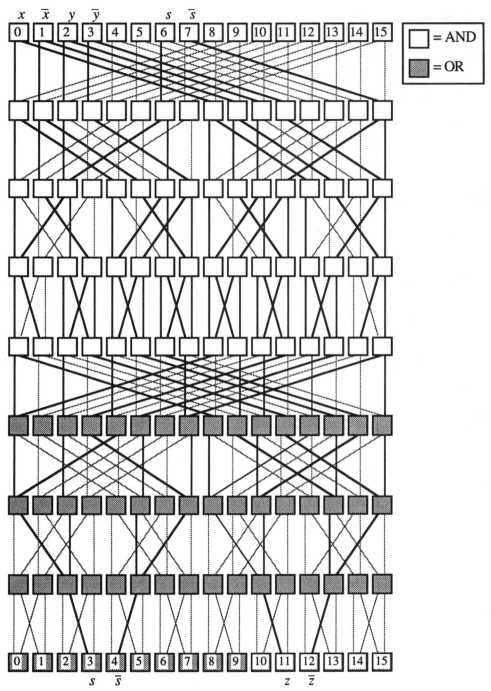

Figure 4.7: *A banyan interconnected serial adder using AND-OR logic.*

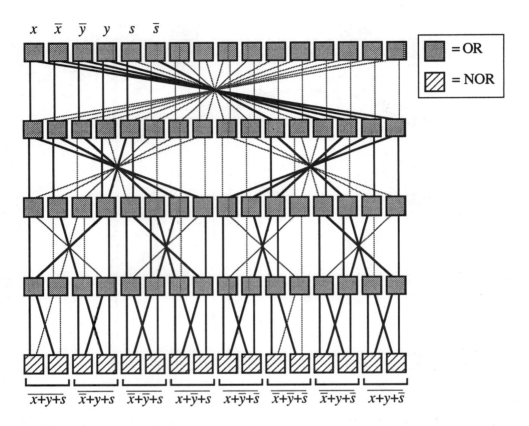

Figure 4.8: *Generation of all three-variable unminimized terms with crossover interconnects and two-input, two-output OR and NOR gates. The bottom stage of logic devices performs logical NOR because an OR-NOR implementation of the AND stage of a PLA matches the operating mode of OLEs. Inputs are provided at the top and two outputs for each term are produced at the bottom. Connections that are masked are dimmed. This circuit is functionally equivalent to the circuit shown in Figure 4.5, except that the outputs are expressed as maxterms rather than minterms. Note that the one-input AND problem has been eliminated since a zero input to OR or NOR logic satisfies the identity property of Boolean algebra.*

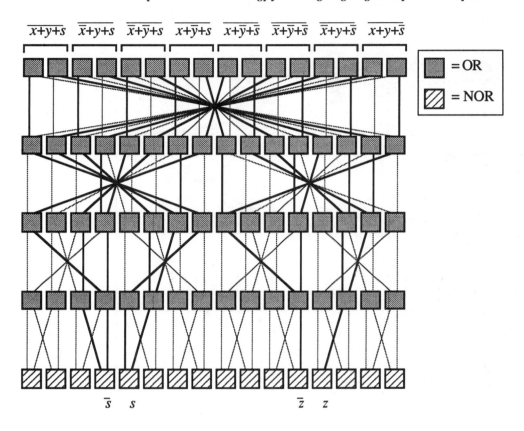

$$\overline{x+y+s} \quad \overline{\overline{x}+y+s} \quad \overline{x+\overline{y}+s} \quad x+\overline{y}+s \quad x+\overline{y}+\overline{s} \quad \overline{x}+\overline{y}+\overline{s} \quad \overline{x}+y+\overline{s} \quad \overline{x+y+\overline{s}}$$

$\overline{s} \qquad s \qquad\qquad\qquad \overline{z} \qquad z$

Figure 4.9: *Mapping terms to state (s) and output (z) functions for a dual-rail serial adder using crossover interconnects and OR-NOR logic. This circuit is functionally equivalent to the circuit shown in Figure 4.6.*

4.1.4 Discussion

Optical pathlengths in the system can be made equal within a very high precision so that the system can be pipelined at the gate level, resulting in increased throughput. This is not an easy task with an irregular interconnect since each type of connection requires its own imaging system, with its own length as well. Pipelining is characteristic of advanced architectures such as the Cray computers [105] where attention is given to individual path lengths. In electronics, differences in path lengths are typically normalized after a few levels of logic with registers. There is no need for designing around individual path lengths or making use of registering with free-space optics because time skews are normalized at each level of logic. Optical power to the devices is available for a narrow window in time, so that signal skews do not accumulate between windows.

Gate count can be reduced by trading depth for width, although the results are largely unpredictable regardless of the interconnect, except for some generalizations about small-depth circuits [41]. The additional cost of using a regular interconnect instead of an arbitrary interconnect for a two-level circuit is a few levels in circuit depth in the OR stage. Any computable function can be realized in two levels of logic with an arbitrary interconnect and unlimited fan-in and fan-out. Likely candidates for optical logic gates [63, 82] have a fan-in and fan-out of about two. This means that a two-level AND-OR equation will need more than two levels of logic to be realized. A straightforward solution to this problem is to organize the AND stage into $\log_{fan-out}M$ levels where M is the number of minterms, and organize the OR stage into $\log_{fan-in}M$ levels. Figure 4.10 shows this transformation for a small circuit, which is straightforward because AND and OR are associative operations. Some candidate optical logic gates may only perform the logical NOR function which is not associative, so the transformation will not be as straightforward. It is a simple task to transform an AND-OR equation into a NOR-NOR equation by adding an inverter level wherever needed but it is a difficult task to do it optimally. For the purpose of analyzing complexity, the AND-OR model will continue to be used.

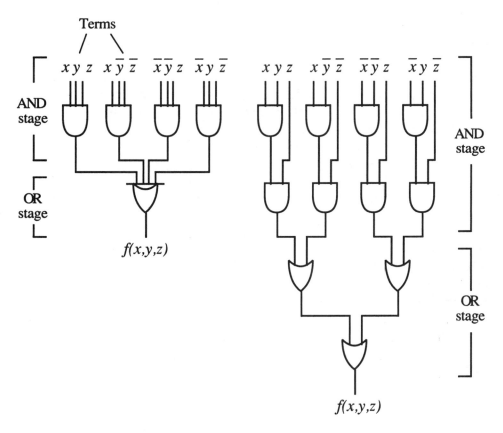

Figure 4.10: *Transforming a two-level AND-OR circuit with unlimited fan-in and fan-out into a $2log_2M$ level circuit with fan-in and fan-out of two. M is the number of terms.*

For logic gates with a fan-in and fan-out of two, the optimal depth of the AND stage using any type of interconnect is log_2M+1 levels to generate two copies of each minterm, where M is the number of minterms that are needed, and the depth of the OR stage varies depending on the function being implemented but is typically less than or equal to log_2M levels. For the design technique presented here, the depths of the AND and OR stages are $log_2M + 1$ levels each, which is a cost of one or two additional gate delays per circuit. A typical circuit in a computer will have about ten gate delays, and the technique presented here adds about two more gate delays per circuit so that the latency of each circuit is increased by 20%. Unlike an electronic design, the speed of the system clock is not decreased for deeper circuits because the lengths of all connections can be made nearly equal, creating a system that can be pipelined at the gate level. A pulsed mode optical power supply guarantees that valid data transitions occur only during the time window that power is present. Each level of a circuit can work on a different problem, so system throughput can be increased by about a factor of ten, since new data can enter the circuit before the result of the previous computation exits.

In terms of gate count, cost is higher when regular interconnects are used. Commercially available electronic PLA's allow both the AND stage and the OR stage to be programmed. With the technique presented here, the AND stage has a fixed form and only the OR stage is customized. This translates to a higher gate count than may be necessary. For example, if we wished to implement the minimized form of the next state function and its complement for a serial adder:

$$s_{t+1} = xy + ys + xs$$
$$\bar{s}_{t+1} = \bar{x}\bar{y} + \bar{y}\bar{s} + \bar{x}\bar{s}$$

all eight unminimized minterms would still be implemented and combined as previously described, and the reduced gate count that could be realized from the minimized form would be ignored. This means there are two additional costs to be considered, the cost of generating more minterms than are needed, and the cost of generating larger minterms than are needed. Although we could simply allow the AND matrix to be programmed as described in the next section, there is currently known no reasonable time-bounded algorithm to do this although there has been some work in the area [20, 96, 109]. The question, then, is how many minterms are generated that are not needed? Dual-rail logic is used to implement functions and their complements in canonical form, so in fact all minterms will always be used since the function and its complement form disjoint subsets that completely cover the minterm space. But if minimized minterms are allowed, then the cost can be exponentially high in the worst case. For example, if we have the function:

$$f_0(x_0, x_1, x_2, x_3) = x_0$$

and its complement:

$$\bar{f}_0(x_0, x_1, x_2, x_3) = \bar{x}_0$$

then only two minimized minterms are needed, x_0 and $\bar{x}_0$. All $2^4 = 16$ minterms will be generated with the PLA technique, however, so the cost in general can be as high as 2^m - 2 extra minterms in the worst case where m is the number of variables. Also, the size of the minterms will always be m with the PLA technique so that in the worst case, minterms are m - 1 variables larger than they need to be. These are worst case estimates and should not be taken as the general case. Pathological cases such as the one just cited do not occur frequently. It is also a rare case that all minterms in the canonical form will be used. If we estimate that each minterm will use half of the available variables, each minterm will be $m/2$ variables larger than it needs to be. An estimate is used because gate count depends on the function being implemented. Using this estimate, approximately $2^{m/2}$ minterms are generated for a circuit implemented with an arbitrary interconnect. Each two-input gate can handle two variables, so the width of the circuit is $m/2 \cdot 2^{m/2}$ gates for an arbitrary interconnect and $m \cdot 2^m$ gates using dual-rail logic for the method proposed here. For the purpose of comparison, an arbitrary interconnect is shown for minimized serial adder equations shown below in Figure 4.11.

$$
\begin{aligned}
z_{t+1} &= \overline{x}\,\overline{y}\,s + \overline{x}\,y\,\overline{s} + x\,y\,s + x\,\overline{y}\,\overline{s} \\
&= m_6 + m_7 + m_8 + m_9 \\
\overline{z}_{t+1} &= \overline{x}\,\overline{y}\,\overline{s} + \overline{x}\,y\,s + x\,y\,\overline{s} + x\,\overline{y}\,s \\
&= m_{10} + m_{11} + m_{12} + m_{13} \\
s_{t+1} &= x\,y + x\,s + y\,s \\
&= m_0 + m_1 + m_2 \\
s_{t+1} &= \overline{x}\,\overline{y} + \overline{x}\,\overline{s} + \overline{y}\,\overline{s} \\
&= m_3 + m_4 + m_5
\end{aligned}
$$

4.1.5 A refinement to the generate-all-terms approach

Narrower and shallower circuits can be realized if flexibility is allowed in positioning the inputs and outputs. The problem we are faced with is determining how to set connections between the inputs and outputs to optimize the circuit along some parameter such as depth, breadth, or space. As a first attempt, we might try to figure out a new design manually, trying different positions for inputs and outputs, and varying circuit depth and breadth. The complexity quickly dominates the process even for small circuits, so the next practical step is to automate the process, and then to add intelligence to the process.

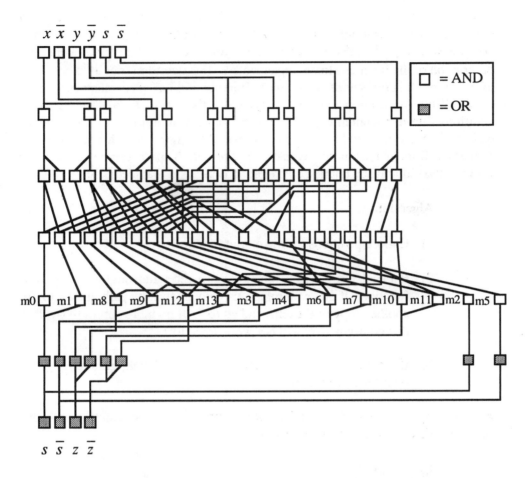

Figure 4.11: *Irregular interconnect for minimized serial adder. 84 logic gates are used in six levels. The input level is not included in the count.*

A brute force tree search algorithm is described here that generates a PLA by trial-and-error. The algorithm produces more compact circuits than the approach described in the previous section but the runtime performance for exhaustive search is intractable for even moderately sized circuits. The algorithm produces a circuit more quickly than a human when a solution does exist to the layout problem presented to it, so the algorithm is described here in the interest of pragmatics. The performance of the algorithm is similar to automated leaf-cell layout in VLSI [94] so we can expect the approach is reasonable.

The algorithm makes a depth-first search through a space consisting of all connection configurations. The width W of the circuit is given and the depth is computed as log_2W. The positions of the input terms are given as well as a description of the functions to be implemented. The algorithm tries all placements of the output functions until a solution is found or until all placements have been tried. When a solution does exist, typically there will be a large space of solutions due to redundancy. This means that a solution can be found more quickly because the likelihood for a successful hit in the search space is more probable. Similar reasoning suggests that the search space can be pruned as a result of the redundancy but no consideration is given to that idea here.

Algorithm:

1) Choose positions for the output functions.

2) For each term of each function, mark the path from the term to the function. If this path interferes with an existing path, then look for another copy of the term and go to 2. If no more copies to try, then this configuration will not work so go to 1.

3) If there is a valid configuration then print the configuration, otherwise print failure.

As an example, consider the complementary functions of a serial sorting node of Batcher's bitonic sorter, described in Chapter 5:

$$\bar{s}_0 = \overline{m_0 + m_3} \qquad\qquad m_0 = s_0 \quad = \bar{\bar{s}}_0$$

$$\bar{s}_1 = \overline{m_1 + m_5} \qquad\qquad m_1 = s_1 \quad = \bar{\bar{s}}_1$$

$$\bar{f}_0 = \overline{m_2 + m_4 + m_6} \qquad m_2 = s_0 x \quad = \overline{\bar{s}_0 + \bar{x}}$$

$$\bar{f}_1 = \overline{m_3 + m_5 + m_6} \qquad m_3 = \bar{s}_1 \bar{x}\, y = \overline{s_1 + x + \bar{y}}$$

$$m_4 = s_1 y \quad = \overline{\bar{s}_1 + \bar{x}}$$

$$m_5 = \bar{s}_0 x \bar{y} = \overline{s_0 + \bar{x} + y}$$

$$m_6 = x y \quad = \overline{\bar{x} + \bar{y}}$$

The layout is done in two parts, one for the top half of the PLA and one for the bottom half. As a general empirical rule, the width of the circuit should be at least four times the number of input variables (twice the number of dual-rail inputs). The layout starts by generating terms for a circuit of width 16 as shown in Figure 4.12, and then uses the positions of the terms chosen by the program to set up the input for the function generation pass. The result of running a layout program that implements the algorithm is shown in Figure 4.12 for the AND stage of a PLA represented in OR-NOR form. The OR stage is shown in Figure 4.13, also represented in OR-NOR form.

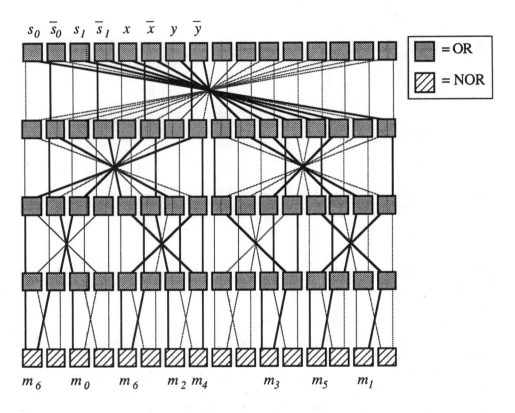

Figure 4.12: *Connection diagram corresponding to the top stage of a PLA for a serial sorting node represented in OR-NOR form.*

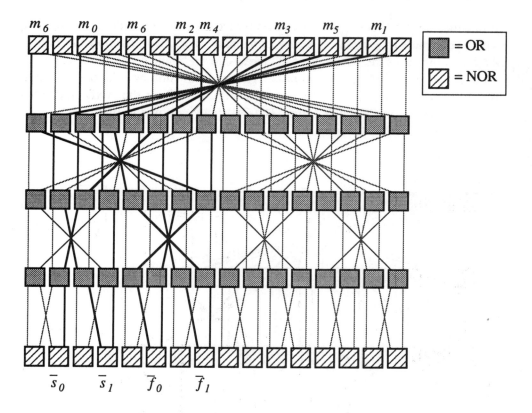

Figure 4.13: *Connection diagram corresponding to the bottom stage of a PLA for a serial sorting node represented in OR-NOR form.*

For this example, 45 minutes of real time was needed for the top stage on an unloaded Microvax II running the Ultrix operating system. Less than one minute of real time was needed for the bottom stage. The complexity of the algorithm grows factorially in the number of output functions since exhaustive search is used, but the runtime behavior is practical for layouts on the order of 100 logic devices since there are a large number of alternative solutions when a solution does exist. The theoretical complexity of the algorithm is not impressive but it solves reasonable problems in much less time than would otherwise be done by hand, as leaf-cell layout in VLSI is still done in many instances. The large number of alternative solutions suggests that a random walk or a simulated annealing approach may prove fruitful for more advanced design tools.

If the algorithmic approach described in Section 4.1 is used for the sorting node instead, then the PLA will be twice as wide and two levels deeper. Although better layout is achieved with exhaustive search, there are some applications where the generate-all-terms approach is preferred. For example, the decoder tree for a random access memory is an ideal application where all terms are needed as described in Section 4.3. The method described in the next section adds enough intelligence to this process to guarantee a fast solution with good asymptotic behavior, although gate count is higher than with the brute force approach.

4.2 PLA design for split+shift interconnects

The optical logic gates are spaced just a few microns apart on an array yet optical signals travel several centimeters through the crossover interconnect in order to interact on the next array of devices. For subnanosecond speeds this latency is intolerable for many applications, particularly those applications that cannot make use of gate-level pipelining. It is not sufficient to measure chip area in describing circuit complexity, free-space volume must be considered as well. A solution to the latency problem is to use a simpler split+shift interconnect that can be implemented with miniature optical components that reduce array spacings. The concept [62] is shown in Figure 4.14 for an array spacing of a few millimeters. The circuit layout has more restrictions because only splits and shifts are allowed, and masking is performed in the device image planes rather than in the mirror and prism array planes of the crossover.

Monolithic fabrication reduces the latency problem but restricts the interconnect topology so that new methods for designing digital circuits have to be considered. With the help of automated layout, new design problems created by the use of monolithically fabricated optical devices and components are effectively solved and it can be argued that the cost of greater circuit depths and breadths is outweighed by the simplified optics and reduced gate-to-gate latencies.

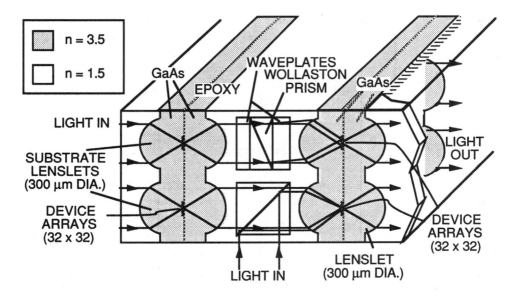

Figure 4.14: *Conceptualization of a microoptics approach for implementing low latency digital optical circuits. Arrays of devices are placed between fabricated lenses that image signals through glass components onto the next arrays of devices. Epoxy binds the structure together. Array spacings are a few millimeters or less. (Photograph provided by the courtesy of Jack Jewell, AT&T Bell Laboratories.)*

Figure 4.15 shows a closed loop, regular interconnection architecture suited for microoptics. The model consists of a two-dimensional input image, a two-dimensional output image, a vertical shift, and a number of logic and connection stages. A vertical shift is provided so that the top row of the input pattern has an opportunity to be imaged onto every row of every mask after a number of iterations. At each stage the image is split into two identical copies, one copy is shifted horizontally with respect to the other, and the images are recombined onto an optically nonlinear array of logic gates such as the OLEs. An image is passed through a mask at each stage that blocks unwanted connections. Dimensions are very small, on the order of a few hundred square microns for a 32x32 device array, using fabricated lenses as shown in Figure 4.16.

When the techniques described in Section 4.1 are applied to the model shown in Figure 4.2, the depth grows linearly in the number of variables and a near-optimal circuit depth is achieved. In general, as the number of variables grows, the size of the circuit does not necessarily have to grow exponentially when minimization is possible even though the minterm space grows exponentially. In order to avoid exponential growth in circuit width for large functions, only the minterms that are needed should be generated. That philosophy applies to the microoptics approach where only split+shift interconnects are allowed, as described below.

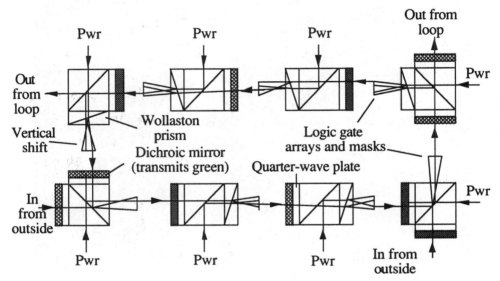

Figure 4.15: *Arrays of optical logic gates are interconnected with split, shift, and combine operations. Masks that customize the interconnects at selected sites are allowed in front of device arrays or behind them. (Illustration provided by the courtesy of Jack Jewell, AT&T Bell Laboratories.)*

The technique described here maps arbitrary logic functions onto a model that uses two-input, two-output OR and NOR gates and two regular connections per level. There are three stages in the resulting design. In the *fan-out* stage, as many copies of the input variables are made as there are unique terms in the equations. In the *term generation* stage, each copy of variables is combined to implement a particular term. In the *function generation* stage, the terms are combined to produce functions. As an example, consider again an implementation of the functions for a dual-rail serial adder expressed in OR-NOR form, where s is the state variable for the carry and z is the output function:

$$s_{t+1} = \overline{\overline{x+y+s_t} + \overline{x+y+\overline{s_t}} + \overline{x+\overline{y}+s_t} + \overline{\overline{x}+y+s_t}}$$

$$\overline{s}_{t+1} = \overline{\overline{x+\overline{y}+\overline{s_t}} + \overline{\overline{x}+y+\overline{s_t}} + \overline{\overline{x}+\overline{y}+s_t} + \overline{x+\overline{y}+\overline{s_t}}}$$

$$z_{t+1} = \overline{\overline{x+y+s_t} + \overline{x+\overline{y}+\overline{s_t}} + \overline{\overline{x}+\overline{y}+s_t} + \overline{\overline{x}+y+\overline{s_t}}}$$

$$\overline{z}_{t+1} = \overline{\overline{x+y+\overline{s_t}} + \overline{x+\overline{y}+s_t} + \overline{\overline{x}+y+s_t} + \overline{\overline{x}+\overline{y}+\overline{s_t}}}$$

Figure 4.16: *Micro-lenslet array photo-electrochemically etched on InP. Lens diameters are approximately 300µm. (Fred Ostermayer, AT&T Bell Laboratories. Photograph provided by the courtesy of Jack Jewell, AT&T Bell Laboratories).*

There are eight unique terms in these equations, so eight copies of the input variables are needed in the fan-out stage. Each copy is reduced to a unique term in the term generation stage, and the terms are combined to realize the four functions in the function generation stage. Input variables are copied in a tree structure so that after the first row of logic gates the copies are separated by half the row width, after the second row of logic gates the copies are separated by one quarter the row width, and so on until copies are adjacent. In the bottom row of the fan-out stage, the adjacent copies allow variables to be shared in the term generation stage so that only half as many copies of the input variables need to be made as there are unique terms in the equations. The separation between the copies of the variables decouples the problems of spatial layout and functional behavior so that the creation of terms in the term generation stage is a trivial process, as well as combining terms in the function generation stage. Only five copies of the input variables are actually needed in the fan-out stage of Figure 4.17 because copies are shared in the term generation stage. In general, this technique will produce good depths and gate counts in a straightforward manner.

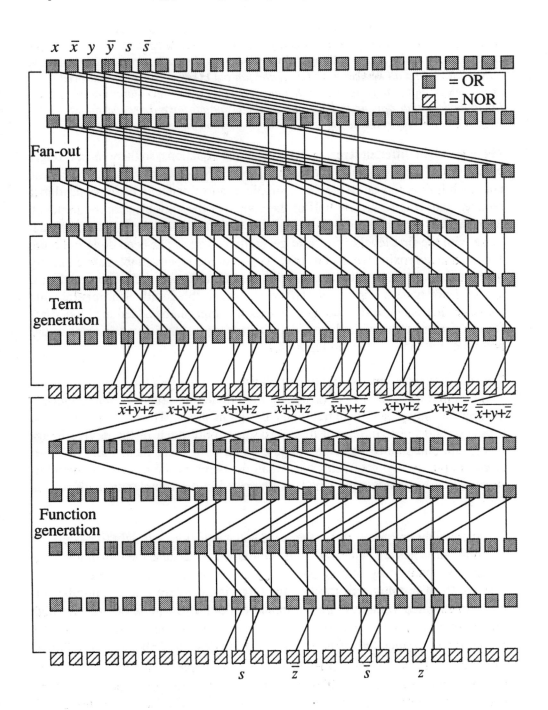

Figure 4.17:   *A dual-rail serial adder is mapped onto a circuit making use of split, shift, and combine interconnects. x and y are the streams to be added, z is the output stream, and s is the carry. All logic devices perform the same function at each stage (OR or NOR) and all devices have fan-in and fan-out of two. Masking is allowed in the device image planes only, so that each logic device has either two outputs or no outputs. Logic devices that appear to have only a single output have a second output that is imaged off of the array due to the regular interconnection pattern.*

There are eight different terms in the serial adder equations, so there must be eight copies of the input variables at the bottom of the fan-out stage. This is the basic approach for the fan-out stage, but a simple improvement can be introduced that reduces gate count. Nearly half of the copies of the variables can be removed from the fan-out stage for most cases by combining the last level of the fan-out stage with the first level of the term generation stage as has been done in Figure 4.17 so that approximately half as many copies of the input variables are explicitly generated. A consideration in using this modification is that the term on the far left will not have a copy to its left to share variables with. In general, this consideration is not serious because an extra column can be added to compensate for the needed term, as is done for the fifth copy of the input variables at the bottom of the fan-out stage in Figure 4.17.

The mapping technique is effective despite the simplicity of the approach, which suggests that the difficulty of designing digital circuits suited for microoptics is not significantly greater than traditional design methods. The limited connection topology and the requirement that masking is only done in the device image planes are constraints that increase gate count by a small factor, and increase circuit depth by two gate delays less than the depth of the minterm generation stage which is already quite small, as described in the complexity analysis that follows.

There are eight unique terms for the serial adder equations but only five copies of the input variables are generated in the fan-out stage because the remaining three copies are obtained by sharing adjacent variables in the term generation stage. The width of a column in the fan-out stage is $2v$ where v is the number of uncomplemented variables, the fan-in and fan-out of the logic devices are both limited to two, and there are 2^v possible unminimized terms, of which only $2^v/2 + 1$ need to be generated because of the sharing described above, so it will take $\lceil \log_2(2^v/2 + 1) \rceil = \lceil \log_2 5 \rceil = 3$ levels to make five copies of the input variables. In the general case only half of the needed minterms, plus one, need to be explicitly generated. The reason is that only half of the available variables in each copy are used to generate each term so that adjacent unused variables are shared. The need for the extra term (actually, just the first few variables) is that the split+shift approach does not allow wraparound to make the first and last terms logically adjacent. Each copy of the input variables contains three complemented variables and three uncomplemented variables, so $\lceil \log_2(3+3) \rceil = 3$ levels are needed to generate the terms, as shown in Figure 4.17. In order to make any combination of the eight terms in the function generation stage, $\lceil \log_2(\text{circuit width}) \rceil = 5$ levels are needed. The entire dual-rail serial adder is shown in Figure 4.17.

The depth of the circuit is $\lceil \log_2(2^v/2 + 1) \rceil + \lceil \log_2(v+v) \rceil + \lceil \log_2(\text{circuit width}) \rceil$ $= 3+3+5 = 11$ where the circuit width is computed as $(2^v/2)(2v) + v$. The "$+ v$" term can usually be reduced to a small number such as 2 as for this case, since only x and its complement are needed for the fifth copy of the input variables. The width of this circuit is 26 gates, and the depth is 11 gates, so the total gate count is $26 \times 11 = 286$ which is a gate count that is 2.25 times greater and a circuit depth that is three gate delays deeper than for the more flexible PLA approach described in Section 4.1. Approximately 1/3 of the logic gates are unused, so a utilization strategy that makes use of the unused logic for other functions can improve effective gate count.

Although the relative shifts in the fan-out and function generation stages are not the same, and the interconnects can generally be manipulated so that the relative shifts are the same, so that these stages can be overlapped among adjoining functions, thus reducing the amount of underutilized logic so that the 2.25 cost factor is higher than it will be in an efficiently tiled system. The exact cost factor depends on the functions being implemented and how well they tile. Gate-to-gate optical pathlengths are nearly identical for all allowed paths between arrays, so that gate-level pipelining is feasible for this approach if logic devices that normalize signals at each level such as S-SEEDs are used. This means that the effective gate count for a switching function averages only a single row per function when the gate-level pipeline remains filled so that the increase in circuit depth does not affect throughput.

The PLA layout method described in Section 4.1 for mapping arbitrary logic equations onto the more flexible banyan interconnect requires a circuit width of $2^{(v+1)}$ and a depth of $2(v+1)$. The 2.25 cost factor for the model described here is small when weighed against the advantages of simplifying the optics used for interconnects, the reduced gate-to-gate latencies, and the opportunity for miniaturization via monolithic fabrication that might otherwise not be possible with banyan, perfect shuffle, or crossover interconnects. For example, the prism array, mirror, two of the masks and a few of the lenses can be eliminated from the crossover setup (see Figure 2.18), to achieve one of the connection stages shown in Figure 4.15. Dichroic mirrors are the only addition but are not needed in the general case. Although the greater number of unused logic gates increases optical power requirements, recent developments in arrays of surface-emitting microlasers [64] allow devices to be selectively powered so that the greater gate count may translate to a space cost rather than a power cost.

An alternative layout method makes use of automated layout that makes a random walk through a solution space of all possible solutions similar to the brute force approach described in the previous section, given the suggested width and depth of the target circuit. The approach is still brute force in the sense that little knowledge about the problem is made available to the program except for the suggested size and shape of the target circuit. The program is effective despite the simplicity of the approach, which suggests that the difficulty of designing digital circuits suited for microoptics is not significantly greater than traditional design methods. The limited connection topology and the requirement that masking is only done in the device image planes are constraints that are easily accommodated.

As an example, consider again an implementation of the Boolean equations for a dual-rail serial adder expressed in OR-NOR form, where s is the state variable for the carry and z is the output:

$$s_{t+1} = \overline{\overline{x+y+\overline{s}_t} + \overline{x+y+\overline{s}_t} + \overline{x+\overline{y}+s_t} + \overline{\overline{x}+y+s_t}}$$

$$\overline{s}_{t+1} = \overline{\overline{x+\overline{y}+\overline{s}_t} + \overline{\overline{x}+y+\overline{s}_t} + \overline{\overline{x}+\overline{y}+s_t} + \overline{x+\overline{y}+s_t}}$$

$$z_{t+1} = \overline{\overline{x+y+s_t} + \overline{x+\overline{y}+\overline{s}_t} + \overline{\overline{x}+y+s_t} + \overline{\overline{x}+y+\overline{s}_t}}$$

$$\overline{z}_{t+1} = \overline{\overline{x+y+\overline{s}_t} + \overline{x+\overline{y}+s_t} + \overline{\overline{x}+y+s_t} + \overline{\overline{x}+\overline{y}+s_t}}$$

An implementation of an interactive random placement approach works well. The user suggests a width and depth of the circuit, as well as the positions of the inputs and the degree of shift at each stage. A functional description of the circuit is provided, as well as a time limit for each trial to find a mapping of the functions onto the circuit. The author spent a few hours in this process to arrive at the layout shown in Figure 4.18, which is reasonable considering the complexity of the problem and the degree of user-machine interaction. The circuit is 20 logic gates wide by 12 levels deep (the bottom level is not counted because it is the top level of the next stage), and should be compared with a 16-wide by eight-deep design of the same circuit described in Section 4.1 using banyan interconnects and separate masking of each split image. For the circuit shown in Figure 4.18, the penalty of restricting gate level interconnects to splits and shifts, and limiting masking to device image planes only is an increase of 50% in circuit depth and an increase of 25% in circuit width when compared with a more flexible banyan or crossover approach. This new cost is small when weighed against the advantages of simplifying the optics used for interconnects and the opportunity for miniaturization via monolithic fabrication that might otherwise not be possible. A smaller overall gate count is realized when compared with the algorithmic approach which suggests that even further optimization may be possible.

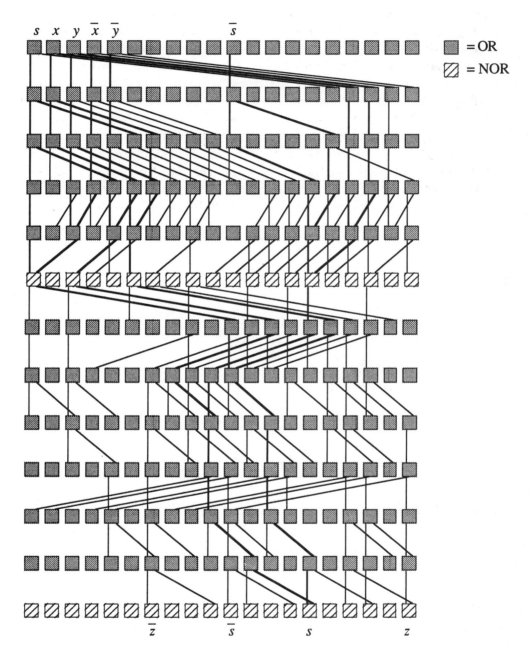

Figure 4.18: *A dual-rail serial adder is mapped onto a circuit making use of split, shift, and combine interconnects.* x *and* y *are the streams to be added,* z *is the output stream, and* s *is the carry. All logic devices perform the same function at each stage*

(OR or NOR) and all devices have fan-in and fan-out of two. Masking is allowed in the device image planes only, so that each logic device has either two outputs or no outputs. Connection paths for function s *are highlighted.*

4.3 Random access memory

A computer memory is called *random access* if any word of the memory can be accessed in an equal amount of time, independent of the position of the word in the memory. Usually the time is logarithmic in the size of the memory. That is, if a random access memory (RAM) contains N words, then any element of the memory can be accessed in $C\lceil \log_f N \rceil$ time, where f is the fan-out (here, we assume a fan-out of two) and C is some constant. For a RAM of size N, $M = \lceil \log_2 N \rceil$ address bits are needed to uniquely identify each word. Address bits are fed to the address decoder of the RAM which selects a word for reading or writing via an M-level deep decoder tree. Read and Write control lines determine whether the addressed location is to be read or written, and data lines provide a means for transferring a word to or from the memory. As the size of the memory grows, the length of the address grows logarithmically, so that one level of depth is added to the decoder tree each time the size of the memory doubles. As a practical example, consider a 100 megaword memory that requires 27 levels of decoding ($2^{27} \approx 10^8$). If we assume that logic gates in the decoding tree switch in 500ps, then a word can be accessed in 13.5ns. Normally a large number of words constituting a *page* will be accessed in succession. In this case, memory may be interleaved so that while one memory is decoding address A_m, other memories are decoding addresses for $A_{m+1}, A_{m+2}, A_{m+3}$ *etc.* In this way address decoding for each word can appear to require only one or two gate delays.

In a conventional RAM an M-bit wide address uniquely identifies one memory location out of a memory space of 2^M locations. In order to access a particular location, the address is presented to the root of a decoder tree containing M levels and 2^M leaves. Starting with the root (the top level of the tree) a decision is made at each ith level of the tree corresponding to the ith bit of the address. If the ith bit is 0 at the ith level, then the tree is traversed to the left, otherwise the tree is traversed to the right. The target leaf is at level $M - 1$ (counting starts at 0). There will be exactly one leaf for each memory address unless more than one subtree is traversed at a time as described below. A four level deep decoder tree for a 16-word RAM is shown in Figure 4.19. As an example of how the decoder tree works, the address 1011 is presented at the root node. The leftmost bit in the address is a 1 so the right path is traversed at Level 0 as indicated by the arrow. The next bit is a 0 so the left path is traversed at Level 1, the next bit is a 1 so the right path is traversed at Level 2, and the last bit is a 1 so the rightmost path is traversed and the addressed leaf is reached at Level 3. If we allow both sides of the decoder tree to be traversed simultaneously, by forcing an address line to be active as well as its complement, then the size of the accessed word doubles and the number of stored words halves. For example, Figure 4.20 shows the decoder tree when the last two address bits are active as well as their complements. This can be continued until the word size equals the size of the memory and the entire memory is read out in parallel. This variation is possible because the storage elements are accessed in parallel, unlike an electronic RAM that is limited by the number of pins connected to the edges of an integrated circuit (IC) [28]. Designs for both the decoding function and the storage function are described in the next section.

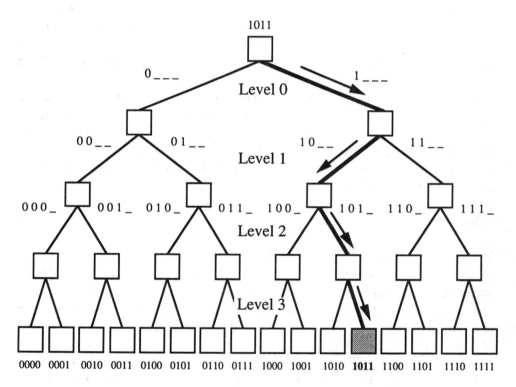

Figure 4.19: *Decoder tree for 16 word random access memory. Decoding path for the word at location 1011 is highlighted.*

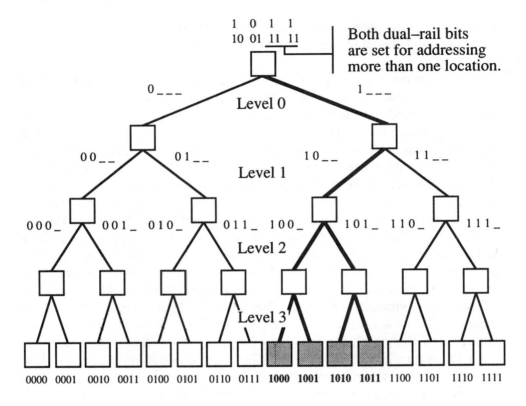

1 0 1 1
10 01 11 11

Both dual–rail bits
are set for addressing
more than one location.

0 _ _ _   Level 0   1 _ _ _

0 0 _ _   0 1 _ _   1 0 _ _   1 1 _ _

Level 1

0 0 0 _   0 0 1 _   0 1 0 _   0 1 1 _   1 0 0 _   1 0 1 _   1 1 0 _   1 1 1 _

Level 2

Level 3

0000 0001 0010 0011 0100 0101 0110 0111 **1000 1001 1010 1011** 1100 1101 1110 1111

Figure 4.20: *Decoder tree for parallel readout. Dual-rail representation is shown for the case when both bits in a dual-rail bit-pair have the same value, which is normally a violation in dual-rail logic. Setting both bits in the two least significant pairs allows four words of memory to be simultaneously addressed.*

Core memory normally consumes a large portion of a computer's hardware, on the order of 10^7 - 10^9 switching components. Hardwired registers consume a much smaller portion, on the order of 10^3 transistors, and offline storage such as hard disks consume on the order of 10^7 transistors for control logic between the offline media and the central processing unit (CPU) with no active switching elements devoted to the memory itself. Conventional von Neumann architectures as well as parallel computers make use of large memories, although this is not necessary for all computers [100].

One method of implementing an optical core memory is to use free space for storage and to use active switching elements for decoding, reading and writing [91]. The result of the design is a near-minimum latency, parallel access memory with less than two active switching elements per stored bit of information.

Access time to any portion of the memory is $O(\log_2 B)$ gate delays for logic gates with fan-in and fan-out of two and a memory size of B bits.

Computer memory generally uses a $\log_2 N$ structure for address decoding, so a reasonable approach in designing an optical memory would be to use an optical $\log_2 N$ interconnect such as the crossover for the decoder and some simple means for storing information. The problem is how to implement the decoding and storage portions of the memory with the fewest number of switching components and with minimum latency between inputs and outputs. The PLA design technique described in Section 4.1 provides an efficient means for implementing the address decoding portion of the memory, and free-space propagation provides an efficient means for storage. The model shown in Figure 4.21 illustrates the architecture of the memory. A two-dimensional input image contains an address and a new word of memory (when writing) and is passed through five crossover stages of varying periods. The stored words of the memory travel through free space while the address is decoded, and then the decoded address and the memory are combined at Stage 5. Stage 6 is the final stage of writing into memory. The new state of the memory is then fed back to the first stage. As described in Chapter 2, in each crossover stage, a two dimensional image is passed through a beam-splitter where it is split into two identical images. One image is passed to a mirror and is reflected back through the system to the output plane with no changes made to the spatial locations of data. The second image is passed to a prism array where data is interchanged according to the period of the prism array. Masks in the image planes customize the interconnect, and an array of optical logic devices regenerates signals allowing for indefinite cascadability. This setup connects the output of every logic gate with the output of another gate according to the crossover pattern, except for connections that are masked out. The interconnection pattern shown in Figure 4.22 shows the connectivity achieved in one pass through the first five crossover stages of Figure 4.21. The logic operations performed by the arrays of devices are assumed to be OR and NOR for S-SEEDs [76] but may be entirely one logic such as NOR, which may result in a higher gate count. This model forms the basis of both the address decoding and storing functions of memory as described in the next section.

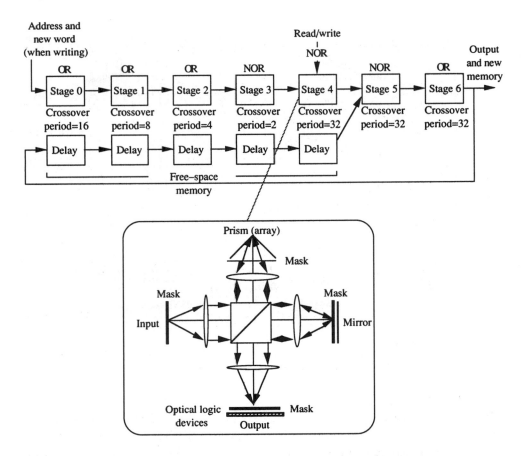

Figure 4.21: *Top: A two-dimensional input image contains an address and a new word (when writing into memory) and is passed through five crossover stages before being combined with the stored words of the memory that are propagating through free space. The output and new state of the memory are produced at Stage 6. A control image is used at Stage 4 to disable the Write logic when the desired operation is Read. Inset: A crossover stage. Connections for one pass are shown in Figure 4.22.*

4.3.1 Design of the memory

The decoding function of a RAM can be satisfied with the AND stage of a PLA structure described in Section 4.1 as shown in Figure 4.23. OR-NOR logic is used rather than AND logic to match the operating mode of S-SEED and OLE devices. The bottom of the decoder tree is 16 bits wide and there are eight unique addresses, so eight two-bit words of memory are accessed in four levels. An eight-word, two-bit memory will be used in the rest of this section for space considerations, but extensions to larger memories are straightforward.

Stage 0

Stage 1

Stage 2

Stage 3

Stage 4

Figure 4.22: *Connectivity achieved on one pass through the five crossover stages shown in Figure 4.21 for arrays of width 32.*

4.3.1.1 Reading from memory

The stored words of the memory d_{000}-d_{111} travel alongside the decoder tree as shown in Figure 4.24. A level has been added to the bottom of the memory so that the addressed locations in the decoder tree are NORed with the stored words of the memory, resulting in the selection of a single group of words. For this OR-NOR configuration, a modified dual-rail address is used. For example, to select two words at locations 000 and 001 (dual-rail 010101 and 010110) the dual-rail address 010111 is used so that all of the unwanted words will be turned off by the NOR logic in Stage 4. The inversion between stages 3 and 4 is cancelled by the crossover which swaps bits within a dual-rail bit-pair so that the positions of dual-rail bits remain intact. The result of the NOR operation is then funnelled through a $\log_2 N$ fan-in structure to a fixed output location on the next pass through the system as shown in Figure 4.25. Note again that the stored words of the memory travel alongside the memory collection tree, because every signal moves on every time step and we must account for the state of the memory at every stage. The memory collection tree is necessary only when selecting a single word or group of words. For full parallel readout, there is no need for the collection tree.

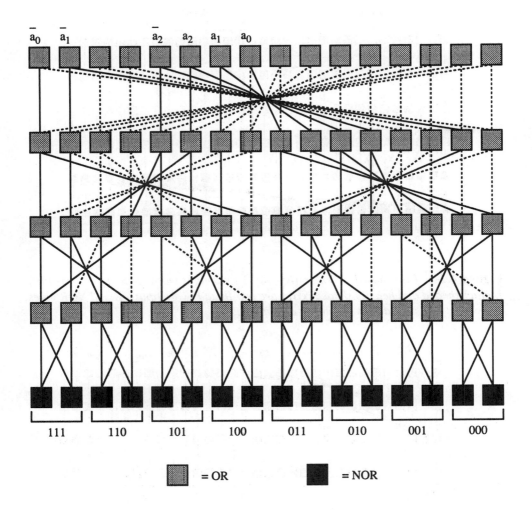

Figure 4.23: *Decoder tree for eight word, two-bit per word random access memory using the AND matrix of a PLA structure. OR-NOR logic is used here to implement AND logic to match the operating mode of S-SEED and OLE devices. Dimmed connections are masked.*

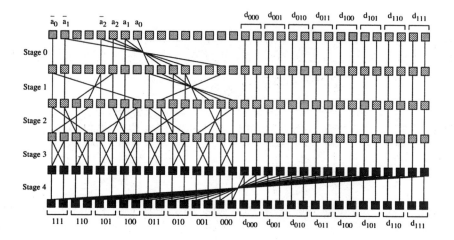

Figure 4.24: *Eight-word decoder (left half) and eight-word memory (right half). Lightly shaded and heavily shaded boxes are two-input / two-output OR and NOR gates, respectively. a_i are address bits and d_j are data bits.*

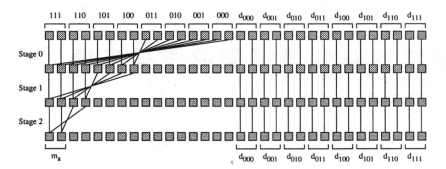

Figure 4.25: *Memory collection tree. The selected word appears at m_a regardless of its position in the memory. The stored data d_j travel alongside the collection tree. All logic gates perform the OR function.*

4.3.1.2 Writing into memory

In order to write into the memory, the old word is erased and the new word is written in its place. There are three steps involved in writing into memory. The first step is to find the addressed word, via a decoder tree. The next step is to use that decoder tree to erase the old value. The last step is to use the decoder tree to enable the location to be written and write the new word into that location. A block diagram of this process is shown in Figure 4.26. The old memory travels straight through on the right side of the diagram. It is interrupted at two locations, a NOR stage where the old word is erased and an OR stage where the new word is written. Since it is not known in advance where the new word is to be written, the new word is written to every leaf of an *N*-wide fan-out tree in the fan-out section. The output of the Decode section is NORed with the output of the fan-out section so that one copy of the word to be written remains, in the proper location. The output of the Decode section is inverted and NORed with the old memory so that every word in the old memory is enabled except for the word at the location to be written. The output is then ORed with the fan-out section to place the new word in the memory at the correct location.

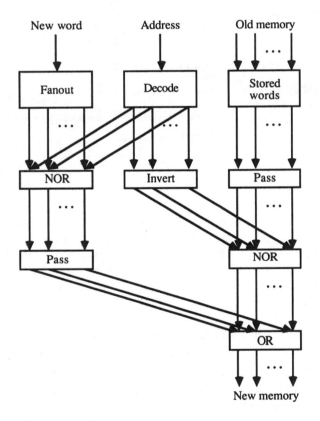

Figure 4.26: *Block diagram of writing into RAM.*

The outputs of the Decode and fan-out sections are superimposed to select one word at the addressed location as shown in Stage 4 of Figure 4.27. The Decode section is inverted and NORed with the old memory to remove the old word at Stage 5, and the fan-out memory is superimposed with the old memory at Stage 6 to yield the new memory. The Read circuitry is superimposed on the Write circuitry by sharing the Decode section and by overlapping the memory collection tree of Figure 4.25 onto the fan-out section as shown in stages 0-2 of Figure 4.27.

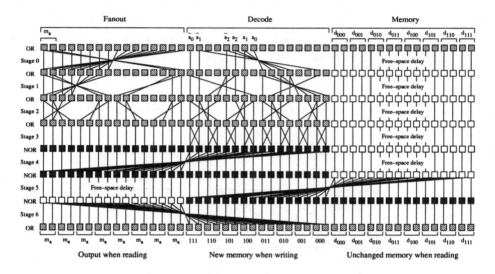

Figure 4.27: *Memory expansion tree for writing into RAM. The Fan-out tree is to the left, The Decode section is in the middle, and the stored words of the memory are to the right. The Decode section is inverted and logically NORed with the stored memory to remove the old word. The data to be written are then logically ORed with the stored memory. The memory collection tree used for reading from memory is superimposed on stages 0-2 of the fan-out section. Unshaded boxes indicate no logic operation due to free-space propagation.*

4.3.2 Discussion on optical random access memory

A typical operation in a von Neumann computer is to read information from memory, perform a function on the data, and place the results back in memory. For this process, the system is wrapped onto itself for cascadability as shown in Figure 4.28. This configuration is made up of a number of logic levels. For a 2^P bit memory, there are $2P - 1$ levels in the Memory Read stage (P levels of decoding and $P - 1$ levels of collection for two-bit words, or $P + 1$ levels of decoding and $P - 2$ levels of collection for four-bit words, *etc.*), $P + 3$ levels in the Memory Write stage, and typically ten or more levels in the ALU. As data travels from one level to the next, activity on any of the other levels has no influence on the level where data is active. Therefore, a different computation can be performed on each level of the ALU and different memory can be stored at each level, allowing the memory and ALU to be pipelined at the gate level. The widths of the decoder tree and the memory are the same as the width of the memory collection tree in the Read logic, so approximately 50% of the memory is consumed by addressing and control logic and the other 50% is consumed by the actual stored words of the memory. For the Write logic, approximately 67% of the memory is consumed by addressing and control logic. These numbers are desirable, since at least one active component is needed for each bit of stored information in current electronic RAM's, as well as additional switching components for decoding so this design is comparable to conventional designs in terms of component count.

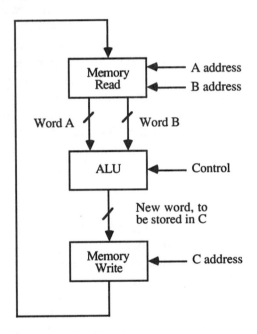

Figure 4.28: *Typical use of random access memory in a von Neumann computer.*

Component count can be improved. Note that when the stored words of the memory travel alongside the decoding and memory collection trees that they do not contribute to any logic operation except where the flow is interrupted. For the levels where memory is simply flowing from one level to the next with no computation taking place on the memory itself, *no logic is needed*. Free-space propagation with appropriate delays provides the means for maintaining data on these levels, which improves the amount of logic devoted to storage to between two and three gates per stored bit of information, the exact number depending on the size of the memory.

There is a philosophical point to consider in designing an all optical RAM. That point is whether or not a RAM should be an integral part of an advanced computer. As the size of a RAM increases, so does the latency required to access every bit of stored information. A better configuration would access large parts of the memory in parallel rather than one word at a time. This cannot easily be accommodated with current electronic packaging technology because of limited pinouts [28]. Free-space optical architectures allow parallel access, and should be preferred to sequential access when memory bandwidth is a problem. The utility of the von Neumann model of a digital computer has created a deep-rooted belief that a powerful computer should have a large central RAM. This belief is not fundamental to computing, and might be dispelled now that new technologies such as optics allow completely parallel access. As an example of an application of the utility of parallel access, consider the difficulty for an electronic computer to move an arbitrarily sized object freely through memory. Serial readout from electronic RAMs means that larger objects require more time to move, but the approach described here for an optical RAM allows for equally rapid access for objects of any size.

4.4 Tiling

A computer is typically made up of a number of subunits such as PLAs that are interconnected in some fashion. It is necessary for the regular free-space model that subunits have the same circuit depths [115]. If the depths are different, then the outputs from functions will not be synchronized and the system will not behave as intended. This is not a major problem for low speed electronics, on the order of a few 10's of megahertz, because the outputs can be made to remain active long enough for an overlap that normalizes the time difference. With pulsed mode optical logic, the power for a logic device is present for a narrow time window, on the order of 10's of picoseconds. There is no opportunity for sustained output signals that overlap in time as there is in electronics where continuous power is used. As a solution we might consider using continuous optical power for our system, but then time skews will develop that will limit the ability to pipeline at the gate level. In addition, some form of clock signal will have to be distributed throughout the system to maintain synchronization.

A more constructive solution is to simply pad the shorter circuits with additional logic or free-space delays to match the depth of the longest circuit. When the differences in depths are not too great, this is a reasonable solution. This is the case in general because circuits tend to grow logarithmically in depth for a linear increase in width.

There are some cases where the depth of one circuit is much greater than the depth of another, possibly by a factor of two or more. Rather than pad the shorter circuit to match the depth of the deeper circuit, the deeper circuit can be padded to match twice the depth of the shallower circuit, or an even multiple of the depth of the shallower circuit for greater differences in depth. For a two-to-one difference in depth, two passes through a short system are needed to implement the deeper circuit rather than one pass through a larger system. Total gate count would either be better or worse with this approach depending on whether the average depth of the circuits are closer to the shallower or deeper circuit.

The widths of the circuits may vary greatly without affecting circuit depths, but there is still a concern that the circuits should adjoin each other with little or no wasted space between them. This may not always be possible because even though we have powerful techniques for mapping arbitrary circuits onto regular structures, we do not as of yet have straightforward techniques for mapping multiple circuits of varying widths onto the *same* regular interconnects. The best we might do in lieu of a better method is to apply some heuristic method to manipulate the circuit layouts to conform to the regular interconnect, or to force the circuits to have the same widths and depths, in which case tiling is trivial if the widths of the interconnects are integral multiples of the widths of the circuits.

4.5 Partitioning

There is a limit on the number of signals that can be passed through a practical lens, on the order of 10^4. A greater number of signals can be accommodated with larger lens systems, but then the advantages of smallness summarized in Figure 2.21 cannot be exploited. A computer will typically have more than 10^6 simultaneously active signals, depending on the size and architecture of the machine. We are therefore forced to partition an optical computer into a number of subunits that do not violate the spatial bandwidth limits of the lens subsystems.

We can take advantage of regularity in partitioning a system. We start by assuming we have a single lens system with a limitless spatial bandwidth capacity. For a practical example, assume the number of signals is 10^6. We take the ratio $10^6/10^4 = 10^2$ which is the number of lens subsystems we will need to achieve the spatial bandwidth of the larger, ideal lens system. These lens subsystems can be connected to achieve the bandwidth of the larger lens system in banyan fashion, maintaining a strict fan-in and fan-out of two and maintaining regular interconnects. The main requirement is that no channel shall exceed the spatial bandwidth limit of 10^4 signals. Figure 4.29 illustrates one way to achieve this connectivity.

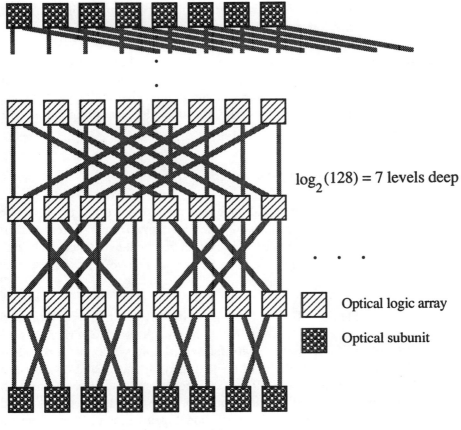

$\log_2(128) = 7$ levels deep

Optical logic array

Optical subunit

128 subsystems wide

Figure 4.29: *A large optical computer is decomposed into 128 subsystems that are interconnected with a banyan. In order to connect 128 subunits to another 128 subunits a network of log$_2$(128)=7 levels of regenerative optical logic gates are placed in between. No channel exceeds the bandwidth limit of 10^4 signals. The banyan is implemented with simple split+shift interconnects.*

The 128 lens subsystems are connected with a banyan structure implemented with split+shift interconnects as described in Chapter 2. The regularity of this structure allows channels to be composed of pairs, so that no channel exceeds the bandwidth capacity of 10^4. New cost is introduced in this partitioning in the form of higher gate count, and increased latency of seven gate levels per circuit. However, the use of a regular split+shift interconnect between the lens subsystems allows for a physical implementation with equidistant paths so that again we can pipeline the system at the gate level and maintain maximum throughput, while satisfying practical limitations of lenses.

Some reordering of the input positions of the subcircuits is necessary for the partitioning in order to compensate for the permuted mapping that the banyan structure imposes on the original form of the system. The reordering does not affect the depths or breadths of the subcircuits since the reordering amounts to simple permutations of the original subcircuits.

4.6 Dealing with faults

Regularity in the structure of a digital optical computer pays off in the detection and isolation of device faults, and simplifies recovery from failures. *Fault avoidance* is distinguished from *fault tolerance*, in that fault avoidance deals with avoiding known faults and fault tolerance deals with recovery from faults that occur after a system is placed in service.

Consider the complexity of a VLSI chip, with several hundred thousand switching components and up to two thirds of the chip devoted to wiring. We are given the task of verifying that a newly fabricated chip works properly. It is impractical to apply test signals to all switching components and connections because of the small scale, inaccessibility of inner layers, and interactions with other components in the circuit. Each transistor cannot be isolated and tested individually, and even if it could, there are data dependent loads that affect the operation of each transistor that might only be known when the entire chip is operating. Some solutions to the verification problem are to use automated visual inspection or to incorporate self-tests in the logic. After the chip is packaged, test sequences can be applied to the pins and the output can be observed for errors. None of these methods is absolute, and at best they detect defects as a second order effect rather than directly from isolated testing. When a defect is found in an electronic chip, the chip might be discarded, or some repair might be possible either through laser surgery or through some built-in recovery feature. Complex VLSI chips exhibit yields on the order of just a few percent on initial runs, so testing has become a significant aspect of electronic digital computing.

For an array of optical logic devices, testing is much easier. Each logic device can be tested individually or as part of a whole array. Since there is little or no electrical or optical coupling between devices, testing is much easier and we can know quickly and with certainty the locations of faulty devices. We can discard the optical chip in favor of a perfect chip, or we can use the chip and avoid the faults.

Regularity in the positions and the functions of the optical logic gates simplifies the problem of dealing with device faults. Interconnection complexity is moved to free space and to masks, which are both generally free of faults. In the left side of Figure 4.30, an array of logic gates is shown with a faulty device in the second row from the top. Some of the logic gates are not used because they cannot be allocated to other functions due to the strict regularity of the gate-level interconnect, and are highlighted with boxes. One method of avoiding the device fault in Figure 4.30 is to rotate the array in 90° increments until the faulty device falls into the position of an unused logic gate. A requirement for this approach is that the devices be rotation symmetric, which means that the devices behave the same in a system if the array is rotated in 90° increments. A rotation into the plane, which results in a left-right reversal, is also a possibility for devices that operate in transmission, but is not considered practical because devices generally operate differently front-to-back than back-to-front.

Rotating an array may not always result in a solution that allows the array to be used. An alternative is to swap the array with its neighbor and try rotations on the swapped arrays. Figure 4.31 illustrates two arrays that have different configurations of faulty and unused logic gates. The two arrays are swapped which places the faulty gate on Array 0 into the position of an unused gate on Array 1. If swapping does not work, then a combination of swapping and rotating may be used. In general, for n square arrays of equally spaced devices, there are four 90° orientations for each array (not counting rotations into the plane) and $n!$ orderings of the arrays, which gives a total of $4^n \cdot n!$ different configurations of the arrays. This combinationally explosive solution space suggests that enormous flexibility exists for dealing with device failures with just these two techniques.

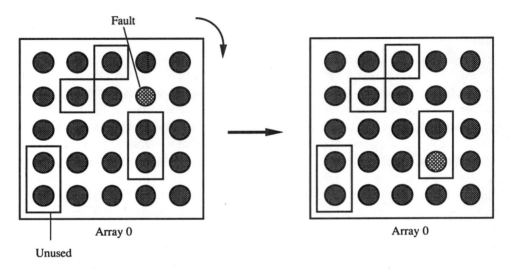

Figure 4.30: *An array with a faulty device is rotated 90° clockwise, which moves the faulty device into the position of an unused device while a good device moves into the position of the faulty device.*

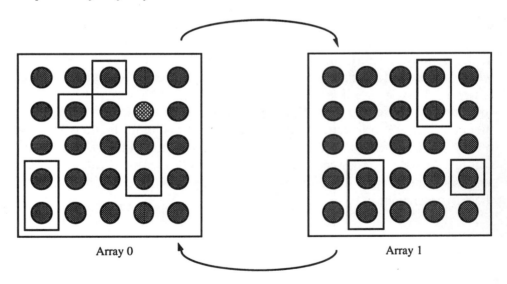

Figure 4.31: *Two arrays are swapped so that the faulty device moves into the position of an unused logic gate.*

It is expected that fast optical logic gates will support fan-ins and fan-outs of only two, or some other small number. In Figure 4.32, it is shown that the output of every logic gate goes to only two other logic gates, and that the inputs to every logic gate come from only two other logic gates. If the straight and angled connections are swapped in one section of a row and the swapping is propagated downward to the lower levels, then a functionally equivalent but physically different circuit results. In Figure 4.32, a faulty device in the left side of the diagram is bypassed by swapping straight and angled connections leaving the right half of Array 1. Changes are propagated to the lower levels.

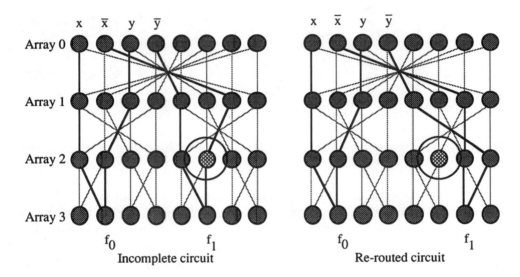

Figure 4.32: *A faulty logic gate (marked with a circle) affects f_1. The circuit is rerouted to avoid the fault by configuring the masks to reposition f_1, using symmetric properties of the interconnection pattern. Dimmed connections mark the positions where masks block light.*

Finally, if some combination of rotation, array swapping and straight/angled connection swapping does not produce a layout that avoids the fault, then a new layout can be generated as shown in Figure 4.33. The time cost of creating an entirely new layout may be large with respect to the cost of simply discarding an array in favor of a more suitable one, so this tradeoff must be considered in modifying a system to accommodate faulty devices.

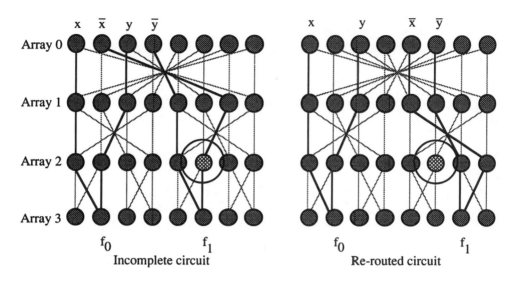

Figure 4.33: *A faulty logic gate affects f_1. The circuit is redesigned to avoid the device fault.*

Failures can happen after a system is placed in service. Some conventional fault tolerant techniques [95] are appropriate for optical computing, such as the method illustrated in Figure 4.34. Two operands enter an adder unit and a result is produced. Since parity is maintained through addition, if the parities computed before and after addition do not agree, then a failure has occurred. The result of a backup "shadow" unit can then be used, assuming the statistical probability of both units failing simultaneously is negligible.

The faulty adder unit might be logically disconnected from the rest of the circuit while the fault is located. The fault can then be isolated by reconfiguring the masks. Rather than fabricate new masks and manually placing them into the system, a method described in the next section allows masks to be changed on-the-fly. The reconfigured faulty adder unit can then be logically reconnected to the system.

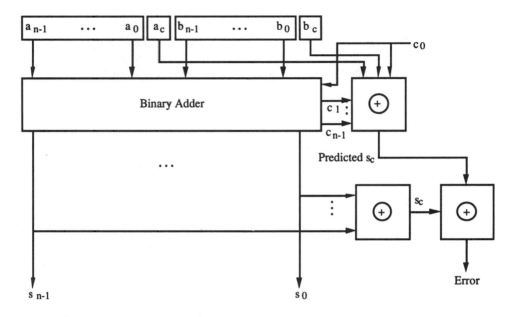

Figure 4.34: *Parity prediction in a binary adder* [95].

4.7 Gate-level reconfigurability

There is no fundamental reason that the masks should remain fixed throughout a computation. When a control sequence is known *a priori* such as for recurrence relations [80], matrix multiplication or the Fast Fourier Transform (FFT) [17] then the control sequence can be generated externally and imaged into the system. The mechanism that generates the sequence is simpler than the main optical computer because it does not need to compute. It only needs to play back a precomputed sequence.

In the system model shown in Figure 4.2 the masks are assumed to be fixed at the time the system is created. That means that the configuration of the hardware is always present even when large parts of it may sit idle. A good numerical computer provides floating point operations as well as integer operations. Floating point is often enhanced with hardware transcendental functions. When the computer is performing integer operations, it will not be using the floating point hardware. When floating point multiplication is performed, transcendental hardware sits idle. When hardware sin() is operating, hardware $\log_b()$ is sitting idle. With fixed interconnects logic is underutilized. If the wires in electronic circuits could be changed on demand, then smaller circuits could be made to yield the same performance as large circuits. There are probably no reasonable means for doing this in electronics, so we may as well put the idea aside as a pipedream. But if the masks in a free-space digital optical computer could be changed on demand, then fewer gates would perform the functions of many, and this we can do.

The opaque areas of the fixed mask in the crossover of Figure 2.18 block light emitting from selected sites of the optical arrays. If the elements of the arrays perform a logical NOR function then the operation of the mask can be satisfied by applying light to the inputs of the logic elements rather than blocking transmission at the outputs. The light that is applied to the inputs can be provided by another optical computer, but one that is simpler than the main computer because it only needs to reproduce a predetermined sequence as illustrated in Figure 4.35. When there is no need for making decisions, then an array of regenerative elements suffices rather than a full logic array.

The need for a second optical computer to drive the first, even though it is simpler raises the question of whether there can be a reasonable gain. The answer is yes, due to the way digital systems are designed today. Consider the system model [42] shown in Figure 4.36. In order to add registers A and B and place the results in register C, register A must be gated onto O-BUS1, register B must be gated onto O-BUS2, the ALU must decode the control lines for the ADD instruction, the I-BUS must be gated to C, and the remaining inputs and outputs to and from the registers must be blocked. Electronically, the enabling and disabling of the bus inputs and outputs is done through tri-state transceivers as illustrated in Figure 4.37. The enable lines must drive all of the transceivers for a particular register. As the size of the word increases, the number of transceiver lines to drive increases as well which limits both word size and speed, in addition to costing additional components to perform the tri-state function.

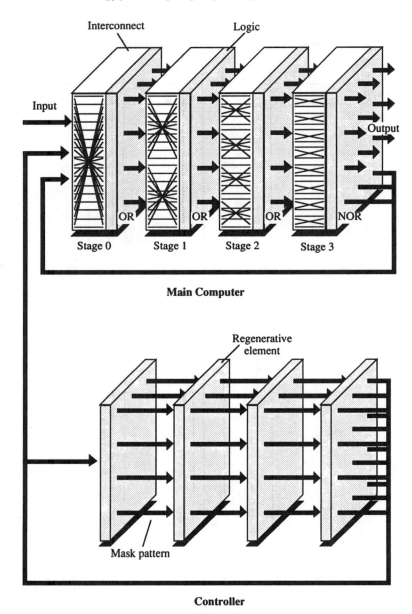

Figure 4.35: *Optical computing model making use of reconfigurable masks. The masks circulate through the controller and are combined onto the first optical logic array of the main computer. In this model, the control sequence does not change over time.*

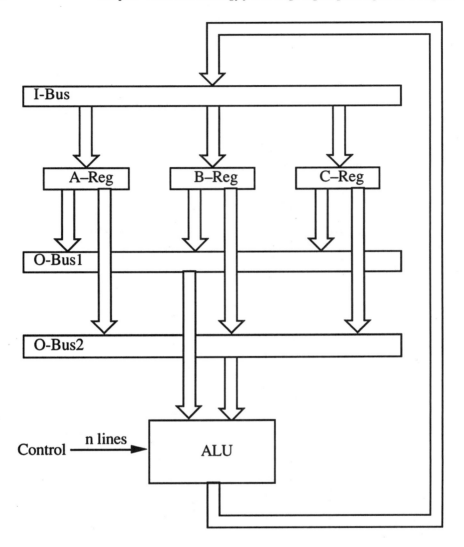

Figure 4.36: *System model for a computer based on register transfers through an arithmetic logic unit (ALU).*

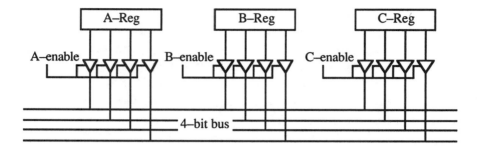

Figure 4.37: *Three four-bit registers gated onto a common bus.*

If connections are changed on-the-fly, then there is no need for transceivers, enable lines to control the transceivers, or logic to compute the states of the enable lines. In addition, latency and component count are reduced as well as the computational overhead of maintaining multiple buses. What this means is that even if the optical computer that drives the reconfigurable masks is as complex as the original optical computer, it still makes sense to use this configuration because the target machine will be smaller and faster than when fixed masks are used.

Reconfigurable masks are not a good approach to digital design in all cases. For example, consider the following program segment:

```
if (a > b) then c = a + b;
          else c = a - b;
```

For the register/ALU model of Figure 4.36, the values of *a* and *b* are compared, and the result determines how the transceiver lines are set. For the reconfigurable mask model the result of the compare, which is a single bit, would have to influence an entire array of $NxN = N^2$ bits. This would require at least $\log_2(N^2)$ = $2\log_2 N$ levels of logic or a different type of logic with a huge gain, which increases gate count and latency more than if just a few transceiver lines are enabled.

A reasonable idea then, is to limit reconfigurable masks to computations that do not branch such as matrix multiplication and signal processing, or Huang's computational origami [52] which is a method of reducing large circuits to a control stream and a kernel, with space and time complexity determined by the number of kernels allowed by the hardware. We can relax this restriction a little to include some level of hardware compiling, where a compiler optimizes a machine description for the object code it produces. If the amount of idle hardware is known only at runtime and is potentially very large, then it may be advantageous for a compiler to include runtime reconfiguration even at the expense of an additional $2\log_2 N$ gate delays. In the long run, the potential for a machine that dynamically reconfigures itself based on the state of the machine rather than in a predetermined sequence is interesting, but for the most part is currently unexplored, so there is a great opportunity for progress in this area.

Chapter 5
Applications of the
Methodology

Design techniques presented in Chapter 4 for regular interconnects only provide tools for designing digital optical circuits. There is not enough content in that chapter to account for special properties of specific systems. For example, in this chapter the design of a parallel sorting network [70, 88] is reported. The sorting network is made up of a number of small circuits that are suitable for an implementation with optical PLAs. Minimization is possible beyond the Chapter 4 techniques for the sorting nodes, and simpler circuits are realized by hand-optimizing the circuits rather than strictly adhering to the algorithmic techniques described in Section 4.1. In Section 5.2, a design is described for an optical implementation of a large parallel computer [39]. For this system, a single optical setup is too small to implement the entire machine so the system is partitioned into smaller units that are regularly interconnected. In section 5.3, an optical design of a content-addressable memory (CAM) is described [87]. An electronic design is severely limited by bandwidth to and from chip packages, so the free-space design addresses that limitation. The purpose of providing case studies for full system designs is to demonstrate that the design techniques described in Chapter 4 are practical, but also to draw attention to the fact that digital designs are made more effective by considering specific properties of the systems being designed. There is still no replacement for a good understanding of the problem to be solved, and this understanding should be used to improve the design of the system.

5.1 An optical design of a parallel sorting network

Digital design techniques described in Chapter 4 are powerful enough to allow designs to be made for complex digital applications [46, 49, 50]. Figure 5.1 is a schematic of an optical computing system composed of arrays of optical logic devices interconnected in free space, customized for a parallel sorting network. A two-dimensional input image is combined with a control array and is passed through five crossover stages of varying periods. The system is fed back onto itself with a vertical shift of one position so that data in row i at time t will be in row $i+1$ at time $t+6$, allowing one time step between crossover stages. In each crossover stage (see Section 2.2.3) a two-dimensional image is passed through a beam-splitter where it is split into two identical images. One image is passed to a mirror and is reflected back through the system to the output plane with no changes made to the spatial locations of data. The second image is passed to a prism array where data is interchanged according to the period of the prism array. Masks in the image planes customize the interconnect, and an array of optical logic devices regenerates signals allowing for cascadability. The goal of this setup is to combine the output of every logic gate with the output of another gate of the same array onto the input of a logic gate on the next array according to the crossover pattern, except for connections that are masked out. Figure 5.2 shows the interconnection pattern achieved in one pass through the system. The logic operations performed by the arrays of devices are assumed to be OR and NOR for S-SEEDs [76] or OLEs but may be entirely one logic such as NOR for simplicity. The use of optics in this parallel sorting network results in an efficient design in terms of gate count and latency. The regularity of gate-level interconnection introduces a small cost factor in gate count and a few levels of delay in the design of the switch, while simplifying the optical hardware by eliminating the need for more complex interconnection means such as fibers or holograms.

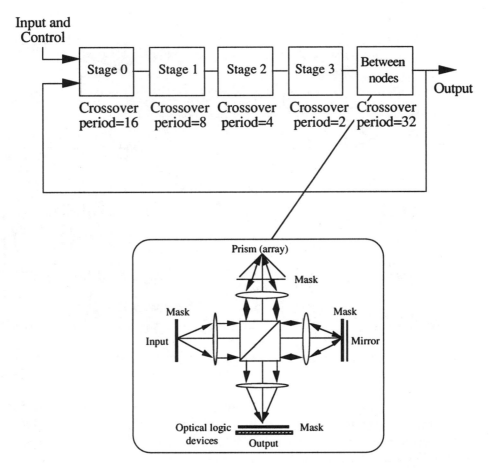

Figure 5.1: *Top: A two-dimensional input image is combined with a two-dimensional control array and is passed through five crossover stages before being fed back to the input. Feedback paths are imaged with a vertical shift so that data spirals through the system, being imaged onto different rows of the masks on each pass. Inset: A crossover stage.*

Period

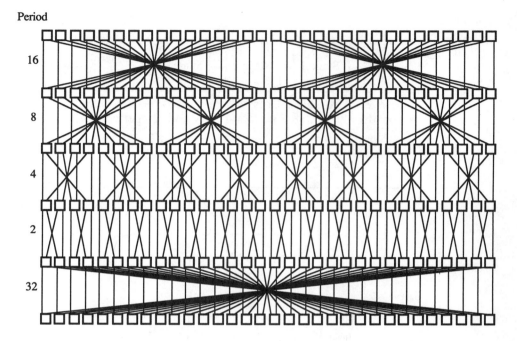

Figure 5.2: *Connectivity achieved on one pass through the five crossover stages shown in Figure 5.1.*

The digital design technique described in Section 4.1 outlines a method for implementing optical PLAs in a straightforward manner using optical logic gates interconnected with space-invariant, free-space optics. An electronic prototype of the sorting network described in the next section was implemented with electronic PLA's so we can expect the use of optical PLA's to produce an implementation with gate count and circuit depth comparable to the electronic prototype. The application of the design techniques to sorting nodes supports the position that regular free-space interconnects provide sufficient connectivity for complex applications such as parallel sorting.

5.1.1 The sorting network

N items such as binary data packets can be sorted in $(\log_2 N)^2$ perfect shuffle interconnected sorting stages [70] of a self-routing network as shown in Figure 5.3 for $N = 16$. There are $\log_2 N$ stages of $\log_2 N$ levels each. In the first stage, $N/2$ bitonically sorted sequences of length two are formed. The first three levels use bypass operations to arrange the streams so that *pivot* bit 0 (the most significant bit, or MSB) of the packet's address is used for sorting in the fourth level of the first stage. In the second stage two levels of bypass operations arrange the streams to sort on pivot bit 1 so that $N/4$ bitonically sorted sequences of length four are formed. The process continues until in the last stage, a mergesort is performed on two bitonically sorted sequences of length $N/2$.

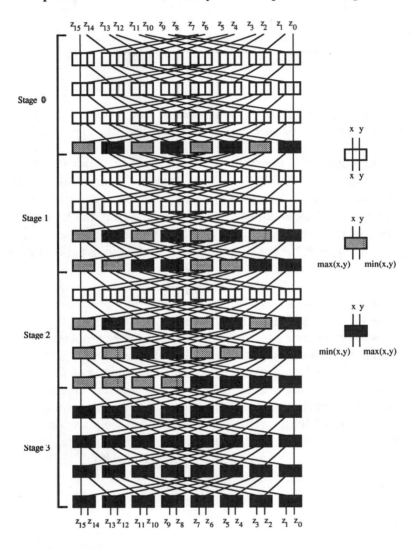

Figure 5.3: *A sorting network based on Batcher's bitonic sorter for 16 items.*

The purpose of the sorting network is to sort fixed length packets of the form shown in Figure 5.4 into an absolute ordering by the destination addresses in the headers.

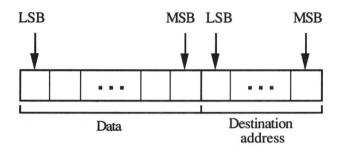

Figure 5.4: *Format of packet. The destination address appears with the most significant bit (MSB) first and the least significant bit (LSB) last. The data follows.*

An electronic prototype of the sorting network implemented with CMOS VLSI technology available in 1983 [92] yielded a per-line internal bandwidth of 20 MHz. Faster external bandwidths are achieved by multiplexing and demultiplexing high bandwidth external lines to and from the lower bandwidth internal lines of the sorting network. The 106 transistors in the VLSI sorting node shown in Figure 5.5 make up 14 logic gates of varying fan-in, fan-out, and logic function. Inputs are at the left and outputs are at the right. Logic gates available in 1983 CMOS VLSI technology are capable of switching in a few nanoseconds, which should yield a per-line bandwidth in excess of 200 MHz. Why then, is this greater speed not achieved? One problem is the capacitance introduced by bonding pads and long wires, and another problem is that signal skews inherent in electronic digital logic [28, 50] are resolved by increasing the time window for signals to arrive at a gate, which reduces per-line bandwidth. This time skew is partially alleviated by registering signals frequently. In the VLSI design of the sorting node shown in Figure 5.5, signals are registered after every three levels of logic. This can be extended only as far as practical limitations allow considering the chip area consumed by registers. For this case, two levels of registering yields a 20 MHz internal bandwidth.

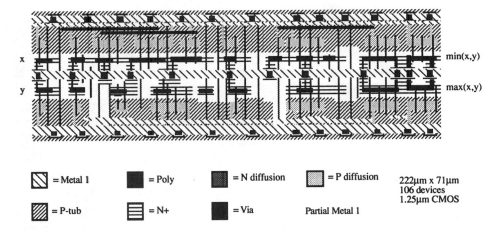

Figure 5.5: *VLSI design of a sorting node for Batcher's bitonic sorter 106 transistors implement 14 logic gates in a 222μm X 71μm area. (Illustration provided by the courtesy of Jay O'Neill, AT&T Bell Laboratories).*

Timing skews are not inherent in free-space optical logic because the use of a planar architecture, pulsed mode optical logic, and regular interconnects reduces signal skews to the extent that gate-level pipelining is made possible even for high switching speeds. One reason for the limited speed of the VLSI design is the large drive requirements involved in getting a signal off of a chip. This is not a current problem with free-space optical logic because wires are not used for carrying data. Pinouts are probably the largest single problem in making a fast parallel sorting network [28]. The input / output (I/O) bandwidth of a chip is limited by the number of pins that can be accommodated with conventional electronic packaging. In the general case, there are not enough pins to match the data rates entering and leaving a chip and even if there were, at 100mW per bonding pad for one VLSI design of the sorting node [92], the heat generated from the power needed for 150MHz operation (a current goal) could destroy the chip.

Since pinouts pose a limitation in present-day electronic computing, we might consider using high speed GaAs electronics for on-chip computing and then converting signals to and from optics for communication between chips, a technique known as *smart pixels* [81]. The idea is to fabricate GaAs digital circuits and then to grow GaAs optical logic such as SEEDs on top. For this configuration, the electronics of a sorting node would look similar to the CMOS version shown in Figure 5.5, but the optical inputs and outputs would be made through electrically controlled SEED devices. This would provide a lower risk entry for optical components into the sorting network rather than an all-optical approach. Only a few SEEDs would be needed for this design at the inputs and outputs, and the SEEDs would eliminate the need for large bonding pads as well as the power required to drive them. Here, we are interested in an all-optical approach in order to take full advantage of the communication and gate-level pipelining capabilities of optics. For that reason, the sorting network design focuses on design methods suited entirely for optics.

There are three types of sorting nodes: *bypass*, *maxsort*, and *minsort*. The bypass node performs a simple straight through connection. The maxsort and minsort nodes are described by the state transition table shown in Figure 5.6 and are shown schematically in Figure 5.7. Streams are passed straight through until they differ, at which point the sorting node locks in either the cross or bypass (bar) state depending on whether the node is performing a minsort or a maxsort.

The sorting node described by the state transition table shown in Figure 5.6 can be implemented in a 16 X 8 matrix of logic gates as shown in Figure 5.8. The network is 16 gates wide and eight levels deep (the last level of gates is not included in the count because it is the first level of logic gates in the succeeding stage). All logic gates have fan-in and fan-out of two. OR and NOR gates (open and shaded boxes, respectively) are used but other functions can be used as appropriate for the available technology. In the last stage of logic, we allow alternating OR and NOR logic at the same level in order to reduce overall gate count in generating complements. The physical implementation still uses identical devices on each array, either all OR or all NOR, but interconnects cross couple the complementary device outputs of S-SEEDs at this stage as shown in Figure 5.9.

16 X 8 = 128 gates are needed for the circuit which may seem large when compared to the 14 logic gates used in the VLSI design shown in Figure 5.5, but other considerations must be made when making comparisons. For example, the logic gates in the VLSI design have nonuniform fan-in and fan-out (one gate has fan-in of four) and implement different switching functions such as exclusive-OR (XOR). If we place the same constraints of fan-in, fan-out, and logic function on both optical and electronic technologies then component counts are closer, although there will still be some unusable components in the optical design due to the restricted interconnection topology. The number of underutilized logic gates caused by the strict use of crossovers is computed by summing the number of logic gates with either no inputs and no outputs or with only a single input and output. For the sorting node shown in Figure 5.8, the number of underutilized

gates is 108, leaving 128 - 108 = 20 necessary gates, so that the total number of gates is about a factor of six greater than what is necessary. The cost factor is dependent on the nature of the function being implemented so a closed form cannot be obtained without considering the function at hand, but an asymptotic bound can be shown for the average case to be within a factor of $2m$ for an m-variable PLA (See Section 4.1.4). Here, m is four.

Current state	Next state / $min(x,y),max(x,y)$			
	$\overline{x}y$ 00	$\overline{x}y$ 01	$x\overline{y}$ 10	xy 11
A: 00	A/00	C/01	B/01	A/11
B: 01	B/00	B/10	B/01	B/11
C: 10	C/00	C/01	C/10	C/11

$$\overline{s_0} = \overline{\overline{s_1 + x + \overline{y} + \overline{s_0}}}$$

$$\overline{s_1} = \overline{\overline{s_0 + \overline{x} + y + \overline{s_1}}}$$

$$\overline{min(x,y)} = \overline{\overline{\overline{x + \overline{y} + \overline{s_1} + \overline{y} + \overline{s_0} + x}}}$$

$$\overline{max(x,y)} = \overline{\overline{s_1 + x + \overline{y} + s_0 + \overline{x} + y + \overline{x} + \overline{y}}}$$

Figure 5.6: *State transition table and minimized Boolean equations for a sorting node. State A is the initial state of the node, state B is cross mode, and state C is bypass (bar) mode. A minsort node is a maxsort node with the positions of the outputs interchanged.*

In terms of latency, there are eight levels of delay in the optical design but only six levels of delay in the VLSI design. Gate-level pipelining is allowed in the optical design for reasons discussed earlier, primarily that optical power supplies are operated in pulse mode which embeds a clock in the power supply. This allows different sets of packets to be sorted on different levels of logic, increasing the utilization of the sorting network. For example, eight sorting networks each in a different phase of operation can be implemented simultaneously because the sorting nodes are eight levels deep. One eighth of the 16 X 8 matrix is devoted to one phase of operation for each of the eight sorting networks, so an average of 16 logic gates are needed per sorting node when the pipeline remains filled which compares well with the VLSI prototype.

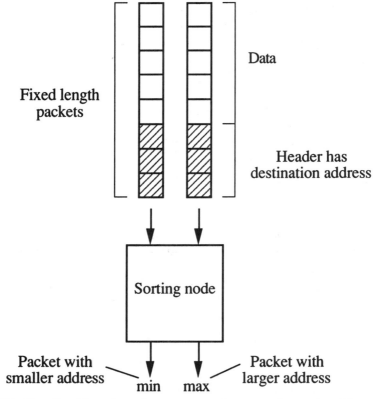

Figure 5.7: *Two fixed length packets enter a minsort sorting node. The packet with the smaller destination address is routed to the left, and the remaining packet is routed to the right.*

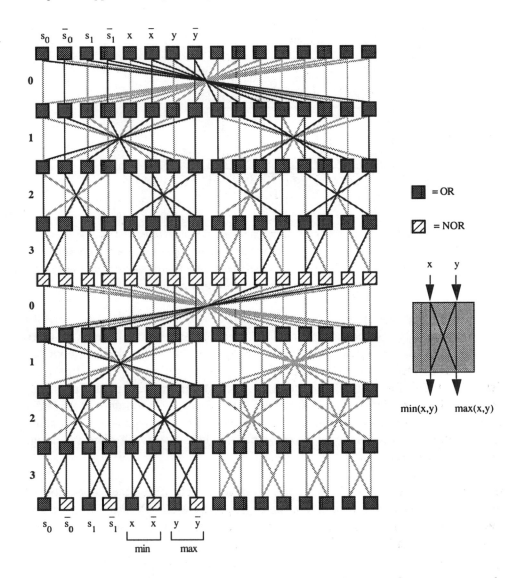

Figure 5.8: *Two-channel sorting node. Inputs are at the top and outputs are at the bottom. Upper levels 0-3 form the OR-NOR matrix where terms of the Boolean equations are generated. Lower levels 0-3 form the OR matrix where functions are generated by combining terms. Dimmed lines mark connections that are removed with connection masks. On the bottom level, both OR and NOR logic are used so that both the functions and their complements are generated.*

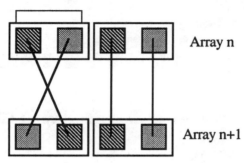

Complementary output
of S-SEED pair

Array n

Array n+1

Figure 5.9: *S-SEEDs are complementary devices, which means that the outputs of each S-SEED logic gate form a pair of light beams where one beam has high intensity and the other beam has low intensity. In order to obtain a relative inversion over just a part of an array, complementary beams within a pair are swapped.*

5.1.2 An improvement to gate count

There are simple properties of optical logic gates and free-space optical interconnects that can significantly reduce the gate count of the sorting network. The SEED device described in Section 2.1.1 exhibits a property called *optical bistability* that allows the device to retain its state after the optical inputs are removed. This property can be exploited for the compare function of the sorting node [112] by latching an exchange signal into either the bypass or cross state without including specific logic to retain the state information. A circuit making use of this property is shown in Figure 5.10.

As long as data streams x and y are the same, logic gate 1 produces a one, logic gates 2 and 3 produce a zero, and none of the gates latch. On the first instance when the streams differ, the exchange output is latched into either the exchange or bypass state. When $x>y$, logic gate 0 latches into the zero state which means that logic gate 3 will produce a zero on all subsequent time steps. When $x<y$, logic gate 1 produces a zero but is unlatched, logic gate 2 latches into the one state, and logic gate 3 latches into the one state and produces ones on all subsequent time steps. The latches are reset externally, such as by removing the electrical bias from the SEED devices.

Advantages of this approach are that the number of logic gates is drastically reduced and the gate-to-gate latency is reduced. In terms of latency, the distance between logic gates is less significant than for the model described earlier in this section because a pulse train can be fed into the circuit rather than relying on interleaved bit streams to make effective use of the logic.

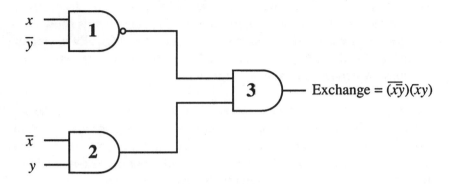

Figure 5.10: *Latching AND/NAND implementation of compare function of a sorting node. The first instance when x and y differ causes either logic gate 1 or 2 to latch depending on the greater of x and y. If x>y, then logic gate 1 latches to the zero state and the Exchange signal produces a zero on all subsequent time steps. If x < y, then logic gates 1 and 2 both produce a one which latches logic gate 3 into the exchange state. Reset is external.*

A problem with exploiting this approach is that latched gates are not unlatched with optical signals. This means that a state machine can never re-enter a state that it has left. For the sorting node, this is not significant but for other applications it is a significant limitation. The latency advantage is not crucial for this application because throughput is unaffected by gate-to-gate latency due to interleaved bit streams, and throughput is typically the most significant property of a sorting network. However, this property can have advantages in other applications that have tight feedback loops.

Gate-level pipelining is not possible with latching logic because the latched gates must be reset before they can compute the compare function for a different pair of data streams, so the overall (space)×(time) complexity of a system making use of latching logic in the sorting nodes may not be improved significantly, but a smaller kernel circuit can be used which simplifies the development of systems and should be considered for that reason.

5.1.3 Discussion

Algorithmic design techniques exist for automatically mapping Boolean logic equations onto regularly interconnected arrays of logic gates as described in Chapter 4, but a more *ad hoc* manual approach is used for the circuits shown here in order to increase efficiency. In creating these circuits, the difficulty in creating these mappings by hand is comparable to the difficulty of designing leaf cells in VLSI technology, which is a common task for a chip designer.

The outputs of one sorting node must cascade to the inputs of another to satisfy the connectivity of the sorting network shown in Figure 5.3, and this constraint has been worked into the design of the sorting node . In Figure 5.11, the outputs of two sorting nodes are passed to the inputs of two different nodes (shown in the bottom "Between Nodes" stage) according to the crossover pattern.

The parallel sorting network continues to scale up in this manner until the space-bandwidth limit is reached and separate lens systems require a partitioning of the machine. This level of connectivity is necessary to satisfy the needs of a high throughput parallel sorting network, and is not readily achieved with conventional electronic approaches. Other optical approaches might be considered such as connecting optical logic devices with guided wave means or holographic optical elements, but then the topological constraints imposed by waveguides and the sacrifice of spatial bandwidth attributed to space-variance can dominate the cost of the design as pointed out in Chapter 1.

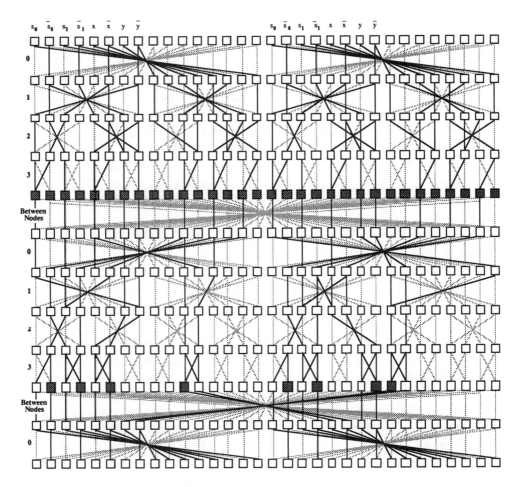

Figure 5.11: *Two sorting nodes interconnected with a 32-wide crossover in the Between Nodes stage.*

Connections between logic gates are customized by masks that block unwanted optical signals. The result of the circuit designs shown in this section and in the rest of this chapter is a set of masks that are placed in each crossover stage of the model similar to the one shown in Figure 3.10. A functional change made to any of the circuits requires an implementation change in the masks only, similar to the way the instruction set of some electronic computers is modified by changing the microcode except that now the entire gate-level interconnect is programmable.

5.2 An optical design of the Connection Machine

The Connection Machine (CM) [44, 45] is an advanced parallel processing computer designed and built by Thinking Machines Corporation. The architecture is noted for high connectivity between a large number of small processors. Free-space optics can provide a large number of regular connections, which is explored in this section in an optical design of the CM [39]. The resulting design is not immediately practical because the size of the machine is beyond the capability of digital optics for at least a few years from this writing. The goal here is to demonstrate the utility of the design techniques presented in Chapter 4 when combined with manual optimization for a large parallel computer. Designs are described for the memories, arithmetic logic units, flag registers, routers, and hypercube of the CM using free-space interconnects.

Section 5.2.1 describes the CM and identifies the significant parts that are redesigned for free-space interconnects. Section 5.2.2 describes the design of the hypercube interconnect. Section 5.2.3 discusses pipelining at the gate level for the CM. Finally, it is concluded that the design techniques used here in the design of an optical CM provide sufficient connection power and flexibility for this architecture despite the strict regularity of the interconnects.

5.2.1 The Connection Machine

The Connection Machine is a massively parallel computer consisting of a large number of one-bit processors arranged at the vertices of an n-space hypercube. Each processor communicates with other processors via *routers* that send and receive messages along each dimension of the hypercube. A block diagram of the CM as described in Reference [45] is shown in Figure 5.12. The host computer is a conventional von Neumann machine such as a Symbolics computer or a SUN computer that runs a program written in a high level language such as LISP or C. Parallelizeable parts of a high level program are farmed out to 2^n processors (2^{16} processors is the size of the CM-1) via a memory bus (for data) and a microcontroller (for instructions) and the results are collected via the memory bus. A separate high bandwidth datapath is provided for input and output directly to and from the hypercube.

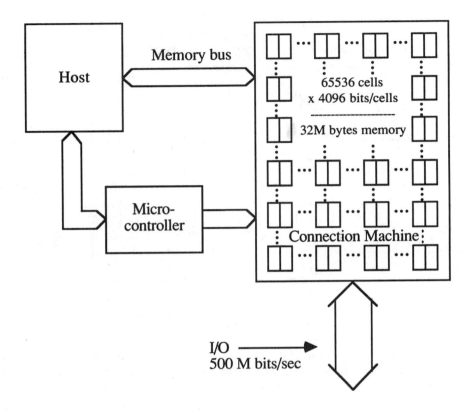

Memory bus

Host

65536 cells
x 4096 bits/cells

32M bytes memory

Micro-
controller

Connection Machine

I/O ⟶
500 M bits/sec

Figure 5.12: *Block diagram of the CM-1 prototype Connection Machine [45].*

The CM makes use of a regular interconnect (an *n*-space hypercube) between the routers that send and receive data packets. The CM-1 prototype uses a 16-space hypercube. A four-space hypercube is shown in Figure 5.13. Each vertex of the hypercube is a router with an attached processing element (PE) that has a unique binary address. Routers that are directly connected to other routers can be found by inverting any one of the four bits in the address. Free-space optics is good at providing regular connections such as the crossover interconnect which can be used to implement the hypercube (see Section 5.2.2).

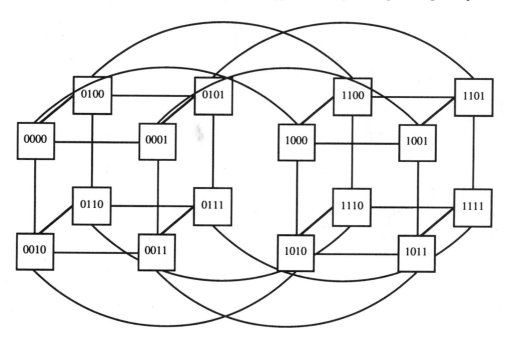

Figure 5.13: *Each vertex of the hypercube is a router with an attached PE that has a unique binary address. Routers that are directly connected to other routers are identified by inverting any one of the bits in the address. A four-space hypercube is shown here.*

Using techniques described in Chapter 4, each PE uses regular interconnects internally. As for the parallel sorting network discussed in the previous section, the use of regular interconnects for the PEs allows pipelining at the gate level, which increases throughput and decreases the size of the machine by sharing logic and memory among PEs. On the down side, gate-level pipelining increases circuit depth and introduces the problem of synchronizing PE's that are in different phases of operation, which is addressed in Section 5.2.3.

Significant components in the CM that are redesigned for free-space optical computing include the hypercube, the PE's, and the routers. Each PE is further broken down into one 16-bit flag register, a three-input, two-output ALU, and a 4096-bit random access memory, as shown in Figure 5.14. This model differs from the original design of a CM PE by dedicating one router to one PE, as opposed to one router serving 16 PE's as in the original design. This tradeoff simplifies the design of the router and makes use of the greater available bandwidth since limited pinouts do not pose a problem for the optical design.

Designs of these components using free-space design techniques are described below.

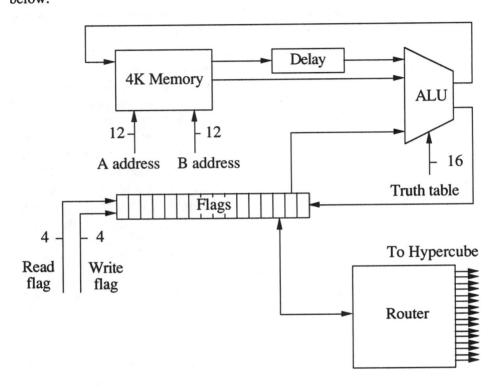

Figure 5.14: *Block diagram of a single Connection Machine processing element.*

5.2.1.1 The processing elements and routers

In the model of a PE shown in Figure 5.14 an external controller (the microcontroller of Figure 5.12) selects two bits of memory via the A address and B address lines. Only one value can be read from memory at a time, so the A value is buffered (delayed, here) while the B value is fetched. The controller selects a flag to read, and feeds the flag and the A and B values into an arithmetic logic unit (ALU) whose function it also selects. The result of the computation produces a new value for the A addressed location and one of the flags. The ALU can be implemented with a simple combinational logic unit as described in the next section. Memory is described in the section that follows. The Flag register is a special case of random access memory since it needs address decoding as well as storage, so it is considered as a small example of a random access memory.

5.2.1.2 The ALU

The ALU takes three one-bit data inputs, two from the memory and one from the flag register, and 16 control inputs from the microcontroller and produces two one-bit data outputs for the memory and flag registers. The ALU generates all 2^3 = 8 combinations (minterms) of the input variables for each of the two outputs. Eight of the 16 control lines turn off the minterms that are not needed in the sum-of-products form of each output. The technique described in Section 4.1 generates a near optimal depth circuit for a PLA that implements the ALU as shown in Figure 5.15. The PLA design technique generates all 2^v minterms of v variables in $v + 1$ levels of crossover connected OR and NOR logic gates, followed by generating functions in $v + 1$ levels of crossover connected OR and NOR logic gates. In Figure 5.15, all combinations of the inputs m_a, m_b, and f are formed after the fourth level of connections (on the fifth row of logic gates from the top). In order to generate a function, the next step is to logically OR the minterms into functions via another $(n + 1)$-level deep banyan structure implemented with OR-NOR logic as described in Chapter 4. Here, the Chapter 4 methods are varied by adding a fifth level of twice the width which contains a different regular interconnect. This is done in order to share the minterm generation logic over both output functions f and m_a.

The regularity of the interconnects reduces signal skew, and the pulsed optical power supply used for logic gates guarantee that any signal skews will not accumulate for more than one level, so that each level of logic can work on a different problem without interference from the other levels. Thus, even though the ALU shown here is made up of 176 two-input, two-output OR and NOR gates in ten levels, it is responsible for implementing ten ALU's each in a different phase of operation. Synchronization among phases is readily handled as discussed in Section 5.2.3. The actual cost per ALU then is 176 / 10 = 17.6 logic gates. It is reasonable to average the hardware over the total number of operations being performed, at least for the CM, because the CM is made up of a large number of identical elements that would have to be realized in one form or another regardless of gate-level pipelining. In a 64K node design of the CM-1, only 64K / 10 nodes need actually be constructed plus some additional synchronization logic that brings out-of-phase PEs back in phase.

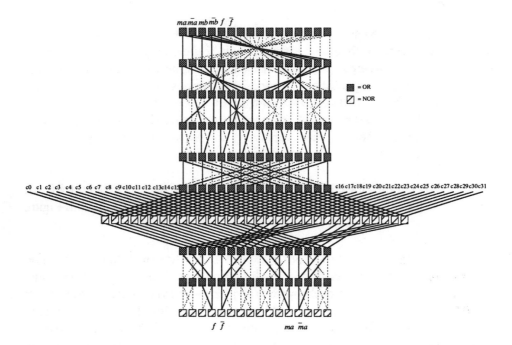

Figure 5.15: *Externally controlled ALU using a variation of the PLA design technique. Implementation is shown for dual-rail logic using OR and NOR gates.*

5.2.1.3 The memory and flag register

The 4K-bit memory at each node can be implemented in the manner described in Section 4.3, so details are not given in this section. Parallel access can be exploited here because the A and B addresses are always the same for all nodes, and 65,536 accesses of one bit from 4096 separate memories can just as well be implemented as one access of 65,536 bits from a single large memory. All of the PEs share the same memory, which is partitioned into 4K-bit blocks for each PE.

The Flag register is a small example of a RAM. Address decoding is needed in the CM flag register to isolate a single bit, and the method of address decoding described in Section 4.3 is sufficient for this purpose. Reading and writing the register is the same as for the RAM. The major difference between the Flag register and the RAM is size: the Flag register is only twice as wide as the eight-word RAM shown in Figure 4.27.

5.2.1.4 The Router

PE's communicate with other PE's through routers. Each router services communication between a PE and the network (for simplicity and for exploiting new communication capabilities afforded by the optics, we assume there is one router for one PE unlike the CM-1 design where one router services 16 PE's) by receiving packets from the network intended for the attached PE, injecting packets into the network, buffering when necessary, and forwarding messages that use the router as an intermediary to get to their destinations.

When a packet comes into the router from either the network or from the PE, an available buffer is identified and is used to store the packet as illustrated in Figure 5.16.

Data to be written is fanned out from the Serial data in line to all four buffers, and data that is to be read is fanned in from all four buffers to the Serial data out line. Separate control logic for each buffer records the current state of the buffer (EMPTY / NOT EMPTY) and is used to generate the Flow-thru control signals that cause serial data to be written into an empty buffer or read out of a full buffer. The diagram shown in Figure 5.17 illustrates how the appropriate Flow-thru signals for writing into the buffers are generated with a PLA.

The mechanism for generating the control lines can be implemented with a five-input, four-output PLA using regular interconnects between stages of identical logic gates using the straight PLA algorithm described in Section 4.1. The Read control circuitry is similar to the Write circuitry except with a different PLA and with a line to the PE indicating there is a packet waiting to be delivered instead of a line indicating there is an incoming packet.

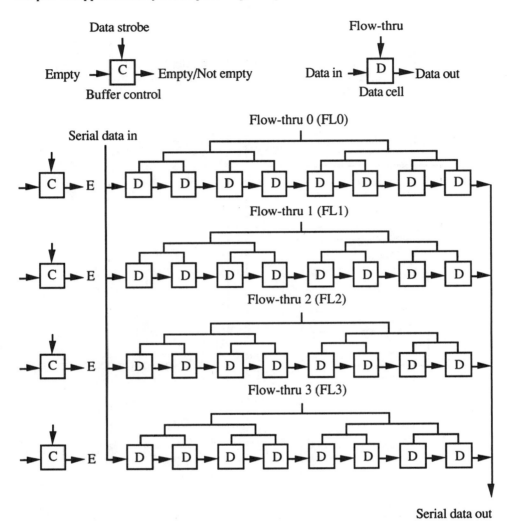

Figure 5.16: *Serial writing into and reading out of four buffers. Control boxes (marked with C's) keep track of whether a buffer (marked with D's) is empty or full. Data enters and leaves the buffer bank in serial fashion.*

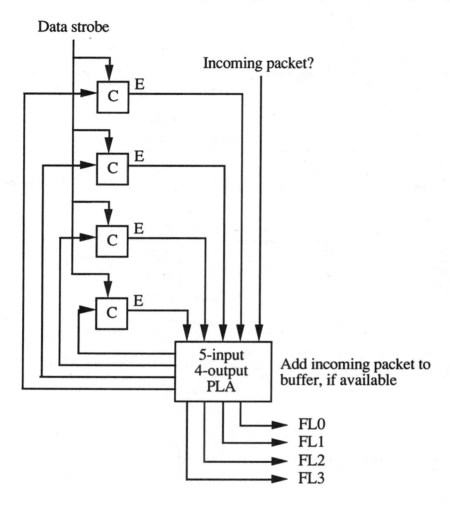

Figure 5.17: *Control circuitry for finding and enabling an available buffer.*

5.2.2 The Hypercube

The 16-space hypercube provides 16 connections, one for each dimension, for each PE. In any technology fan-in and fan-out are limited to a number typically less than 16, so that 16-dimensional connectivity requires more than one level of logic or regeneration. Here, we assume fan-in and fan-out are both limited to two so that 16-space connectivity is achieved in no less than $\lceil \log_2 16 \rceil$ levels regardless of the means used for interconnection. A banyan or crossover can be used as the $\lceil \log_2 16 \rceil$ interconnection pattern for the input and output trees of a 16-space hypercube vertex as shown in Figure 5.18, where one leaf node of each tree connects the PE to one of the 16 dimensions of the hypercube. The upper half of the diagram shows the incoming $\lceil \log_2 16 \rceil = 4$-level crossover equivalent of the 16-space hypercube vertex while the bottom half shows the outgoing crossover equivalent hypercube vertex. A hypercube interconnect can be realized with crossovers in a comparable component count as would be needed for a direct implementation given the same fan-in and fan-out constraints, for machines with small dimensionality ($\approx$ 16).

We cannot implement the entire CM hypercube with one optical logic array, so we are forced to partition the hypercube over a number of arrays. In order to partition the hypercube without adding significant cost to the design, we can use the property that a large perfect shuffle (or nearly any other $\log_2 N$ interconnect such as the crossover) can be realized with a perfect shuffle of smaller shuffles. Figure 5.19 shows a 16-wide shuffle implemented with four four-wide shuffles that are shuffled together. The full connectivity of the original shuffle is still realized, but the cost of an additional stage of logic has been added. In general, this cost adds up to one stage of logic for each decomposition of the shuffle. There are on the order of 2^{30} switching components in the CM-1 and about 2^{14} switching components can be expected in an optical array, which means that approximately $2^{30} / 2^{14} = 2^{16}$ arrays will be needed. An array corresponds roughly to an electronic integrated circuit in terms of complexity, so the 2^{16} array figure is not ridiculous considering the CM-1 needs the same complexity and costs several million dollars. In the worst case, every array will need to be connected to every other, so that $\log_2(2^{14}) = 16$ additional levels will be needed across the entire hypercube to compensate for the fact that 2^{30} components cannot be placed on a single array. This cost of 16 gate delays is quite small when compared with the size of the entire machine and when consideration is made that this cost may be the most significant packaging constraint, unlike electronic technologies where capacitance and inductance from densely packed conductors pose primary limitations on speed that introduce a cost of much more than 16 gate delays (see Section 1.3).

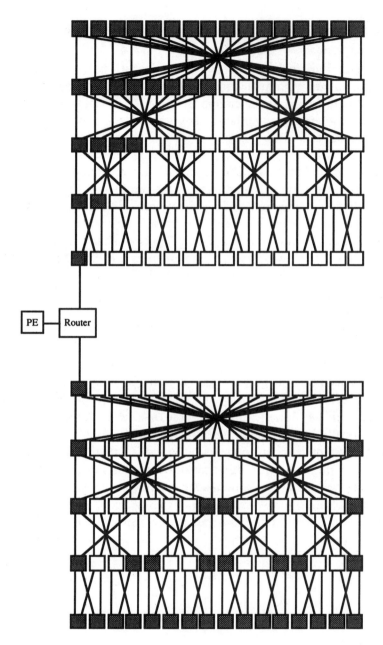

Figure 5.18: *Crossover connection pattern at a vertex of a 16-space hypercube. Upper half is the incoming network, bottom half is the outgoing network. Shaded boxes indicate nodes that make up the crossover equivalent hypercube. There is one input/output box for each dimension of the hypercube.*

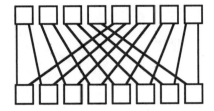

1-level, 8 node perfect shuffle

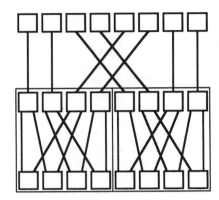

1-level, 8 node perfect shuffle
implemented as a 4-shuffle of two
4-node shuffles

Figure 5.19: *A 16-channel perfect shuffle is realized as a perfect shuffle of two 8-channel perfect shuffles. The top level shuffle and the two 8-channel shuffles steer light in less than eight directions each, whereas the 16-channel shuffle steers light in 16 directions, which makes the 2-level shuffle easier to decompose optically.*

5.2.3 Discussion

Every PE must be equally accessible to every other PE via routers, so that PE's that are pipelined at the gate level must be synchronized because they are in different phases of operation. Figure 5.20 shows how this can be done using a fan-out tree with optical delays. The output of the eight-level logic unit is fed to a delay tree, where each output is marked in the diagram by the amount of delay along that path. The cost of the fan-out tree is 15 times the width of the circuit, and in general the cost is $(2n - 1) \times$(circuit width) gates for an n-level deep circuit. The increased latency is $\log_2 n$ levels, while the saving in system gate count is $(n^2 - 3n + 1) \times$(circuit width) since n circuits are implemented with only $(n + 2n - 1) \times$(circuit width) logic gates rather than the $(n \times n) \times$(circuit width) logic gates that would otherwise be required. This tradeoff is made possible here because of the large number of identical logic units in the CM. In this way, the additional gate count caused by the strict use of regular interconnects at the gate level is offset by the savings gained in gate-level pipelining.

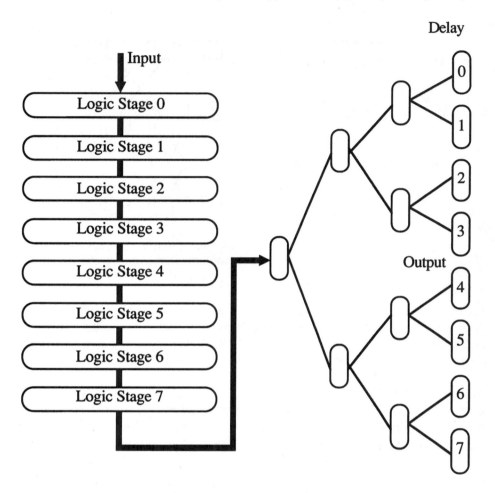

Figure 5.20: *An eight-level pipelined logic unit.*

The optical Connection Machine project covered in this section was funded in part by the Air Force Office of Scientific Research under grant AFOSR-86-0294.

5.3 An optical design of a content addressable memory

A design of a content addressable memory (CAM) [27] is described here that demands high throughput that cannot be satisfied with a conventional electronic approach. Optics is a suitable approach for this application because connectivity is dense, and in an electronic implementation bandwidth between chips must be as great as bandwidth between devices on the chips to avoid sacrificing throughput. The optical design proposed here meets the high density and high throughput goals for the CAM.

5.3.1 Background on CAM

In a random access memory (RAM) each word of memory has a unique address. The physical position of a word in the memory is as significant as the value of the word. In a content addressable memory (CAM) a word is composed of *fields* that can be used as keys for indexing into the memory. The physical location of a CAM word is generally not as significant as the values contained in the fields of the word. Relationships between addresses, values and fields for RAM and CAM are shown in Figure 5.21. Values are stored in sequential locations in the RAM, with the address acting as the key to find the word. Four-byte address increments are used in this example. Values are stored in fields in the CAM, and in principle any field can be used to key on the rest of the word. If the CAM words are reordered, then the contents of the CAM are virtually unchanged since physical location has no bearing on the interpretation of the fields. A reordering of the RAM may change the meanings of its values entirely. This comparison suggests that CAM may be a preferred means for storing information when there is a significant cost with maintaining data in sorted order.

Random access memory		Content addressable memory		
Address	Value	Field1	Field2	Field3
0000A000	0F0F0000	000	A	9E
0000A004	186734F1	011	0	F0
0000A008	0F000000	149	7	01
0000A00C	FE681022	091	4	00
0000A010	3152467C	000	E	FE
0000A014	C3450917	749	C	6E
0000A018	00392B11	000	0	50
0000A01C	10034561	575	1	84
32 bits	32 bits	12 bits	4 bits	8 bits

Figure 5.21: *Relationships between random access memory and content addressable memory. The random access memory associates a value with a unique address. The content addressable memory associates data by fields.*

When a search is made through a RAM for a particular value, the entire memory may need to be searched, a single word at a time for the value when the memory is not sorted. When the RAM is maintained in sorted order, a number of accesses may still be acquired to either find the value being searched or to determine the value is not stored in the memory. In a CAM, the value being searched is broadcast to all of the words simultaneously, and a small processor at each word makes a field comparison for membership, and in two steps the answer is known. A few additional steps may be needed to collect the results but in general the time required to search a CAM is less than for a RAM in the same technology, for a number of applications.

CAM's are not in common use largely due to the difficulty of implementing an efficient design with conventional technology. Consider the block diagram of a CAM shown in Figure 5.22 [27]. A Central Control unit sends a comparand to each of 4096 cells, where a comparison is made and the result is put in the Tag bits T_i which are collected by a Data Gathering Device and sent to the Central Control unit. When the Central Control unit loads the value to be searched into the comparand register, it sets up a mask to block out fields that are not part of the value. A small local processor in each cell makes a comparison between its local word and the broadcast value and reports the result of the comparison to the Data Gathering Device.

A number of problems arise when an attempt is made to implement this architecture in a conventional technology such as VLSI. The broadcast function that sends the comparand to the cells can be implemented with low latency if a tree structure is used. An H-tree [80] can be used for the tree layout if it will fit on a single integrated circuit (IC). If the tree cannot be contained on a single chip, then connections must be made among a number of chips, which quickly limits chip density [28]. For example, a node of a tree that has a single four-bit input and two four-bit outputs needs 12 input/output (I/O) pins and three control pins if only one node is placed on a chip. A three node subtree needs 25 pins and a seven node subtree needs 45 pins as shown in Figure 5.23. A 63 node subtree requires 325 pins, excluding power and control pins, and this outstrips most present day packaging technologies. A useful CAM would contain thousands of such nodes with wider data paths, so the I/O bandwidth limit is realized early in the design of the CAM. Compromises can be made by multiplexing data onto the limited number of I/O connections but this reduces effective speed which is a major reason for using a CAM. The goal here is to show that a CAM can be efficiently implemented with optical logic devices and regular free-space optical interconnects.

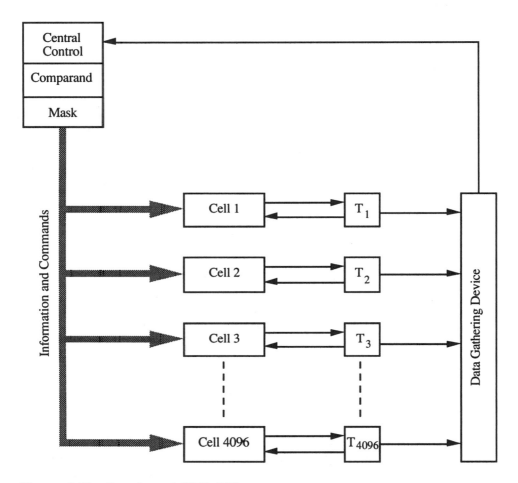

Figure 5.22: *Overview of CAM [27].*

5.3.2 Functional layout of the CAM

The layout of a CAM developed at Rutgers University [87] is shown in Figure 5.24. A conventional RAM, a Register File, an Instruction Unit, and a Logic Unit make up a simple computer. A distribution and collection tree, the CAM words, and a Backing Store for the CAM words make up an extension to the simple computer. The Instruction Unit acts as the central control for the system. An instruction is sent from the Instruction Unit to the Logic Unit, where the instruction is decoded into microcode sequences that are distributed via a tree structure to all of the CAM cells in the tree. A Backing Store made up of serial memory extends the width of a CAM word without introducing significant cost

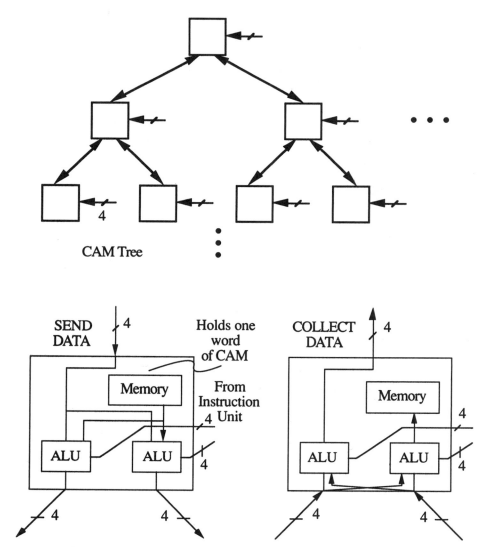

Figure 5.25: *A node in the CAM tree contains two ALU's, enough memory to hold one CAM word, and bidirectional links for sending and collecting data.*

A block diagram of an ALU based on the 74181 is illustrated in Figure 5.26. A four-bit instruction channel S and a mode input M control the operation of the three data channels A, B, and C. Inputs and outputs for serial carry and carry lookahead are provided as well. An optical design for this element and the supporting circuitry are described in the next section.

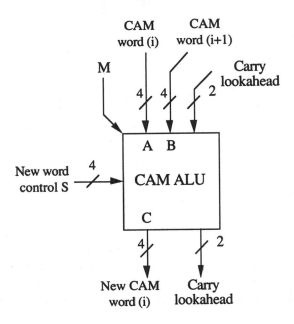

Figure 5.26: *Four-bit 74181 arithmetic logic unit/function generator.*

5.3.3 Regular interconnect design

The ALU's are similar in function and design to the Texas Instruments 74181 four-bit ALU chip. The 74181 is made up of four one-bit sections that operate in parallel for carryless operations and operate in parallel/serial mode for carry operations. The regular interconnect design for a one-bit section is shown in Figures 5.27 and 5.28. The target optical architecture for the ALU is made up of cascadable arrays of two-input, two-output NOR gates interconnected in free space with a regular interconnection scheme such as shown in Figure 3.10. The reason that only NOR logic is used is that this design is intended for a physical implementation that uses all NOR logic as described in Chapter 6. The restricted interconnection topology does not introduce a large cost in space or time as the reader might now expect.

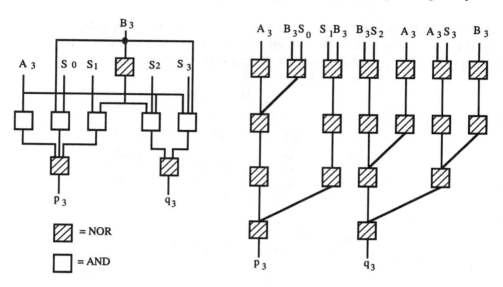

Figure 5.27: *Functional layout of top half of 74181 one-bit unit which uses an irregular interconnection pattern, large fan-in, and mixed-mode logic (left side of diagram) and two-input, two-output NOR equivalent making use of regular interconnection patterns (right side). A and B are four-bit input words, S is the control word, and p and q are intermediate results used in the bottom half of the structure shown in Figure 5.28.*

The backing store can be implemented efficiently with four-bit wide serial delay lines since the four-bit ALUs can only process data in four-bit nibbles stored sequentially in this design. A block diagram illustrates this in Figure 5.29. The linear distance between the output of the Read/Write mechanism and the input from the feedback path is great enough to store a large word (on the order of several hundred bits), in delay logic or in free space as it propagates around the feedback loop.

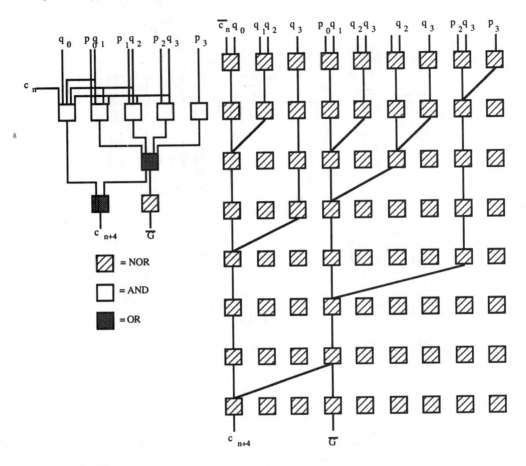

Figure 5.28: *Functional layout of bottom half of 74181 one-bit unit (left side of diagram) and two-input, two-output NOR equivalent using regular interconnection patterns (right side). p and q are intermediate results computed in the top half of the structure as shown in Figure 5.27. c_n is the carry, and G is the output. The top three stages of the regular interconnect design use the same interconnection pattern that is used for the top half shown in Figure 5.27.*

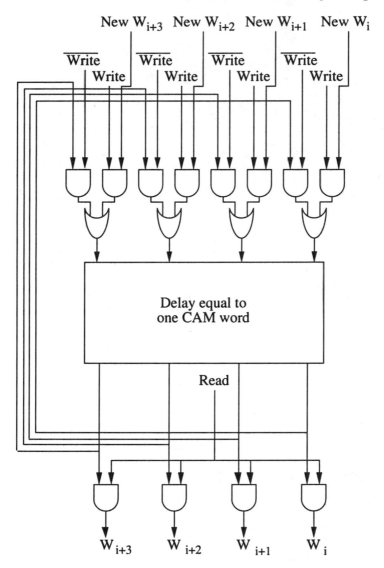

Figure 5.29: *Read/Write mechanism for four-bit wide delay memory for CAM word and Backing Store.*

The tree connections between PE's can be implemented with a cascadable optical perfect shuffle (or a topologically equivalent crossover network) as shown in Figure 5.30. Designs for the remaining components are not included here since conventional electronic technology is used.

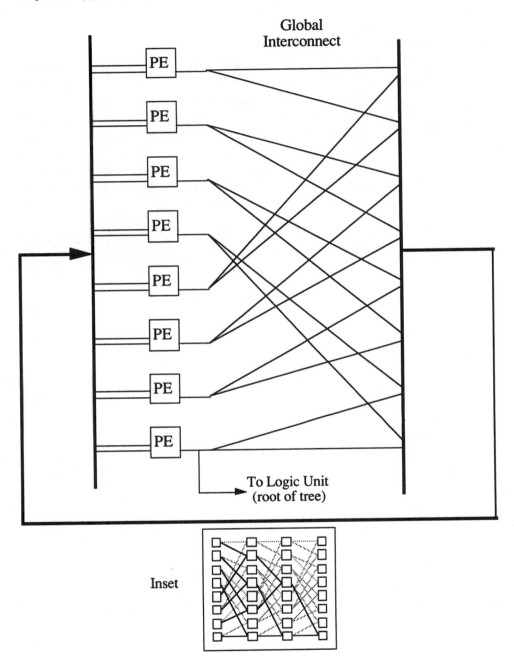

Figure 5.30: *A perfect shuffle interconnect (or the topologically equivalent crossover interconnect) implements a tree data collection scheme. Inset: Highlighted connections show connectivity of the tree.*

5.3.4 Discussion

In this chapter, optical designs for a parallel sorting network, the Connection Machine, and a content addressable memory were discussed. The designs make use of arrays of optically nonlinear logic gates interconnected in free space using digital design techniques described in Chapter 4, augmented with hand optimization to take advantage of properties of the architectures being designed. The designs are good candidates for optical implementations because the bandwidth requirements cannot be met with electronics technology in the foreseeable future, and because the optical interconnection schemes are suitable for a physical implementation as described in the next chapter.

The Optical CAM project covered in this section was funded in part by the Air Force Office of Scientific Research under grant AFOSR-86-0294.

Chapter 6
Summary

Currently, price to performance ratios favor electronic digital computing. Optical power produced by semiconductor lasers is thousands of times more expensive than electrical power, optical logic device processing is less advanced than electronic VLSI and electronic GaAs, bulk optical components such as lenses and prisms are relatively expensive, and it is time consuming to design and implement optical systems. Given the costs associated with optical computing, we should ask ourselves, "Do we really need more powerful computers?" The answer is "Yes."

There exist important applications with needs that cannot be met with present day computer hardware, and may never be satisfied unless some radical changes are made in the way communication is managed [43]. Examples of these applications [57, 100] are weather prediction [84], wind tunnel modeling, high bandwidth switching, artificial intelligence [45, 47], and analysis of remotely sensed data where supercomputers like the Crays find their use today. Other applications include traffic management and multimedia databases [22], and neural networks [33, 78, 104]. Of these applications, high bandwidth switching will affect nearly everyone. A single wideband digital switch can be used as a central telephone office switch serving voice, data, and video needs for a small city. In the full implementation of AT&T's Starlite wideband digital switch [54], people at home and at work receive and send packetized voice, data, and video in one-to-one, one-to-many, many-to-one, and many-to-many configurations. Rather than receiving a small set of broadcast video signals from the local cable television company, end users can request video services which are satisfied on demand by a network of wideband digital switches. End users can also become broadcasters, and engage in video calls and data services at will. Long term design goals for an electronic implementation of the switch cannot be met with conventional technology, at least partly due to the limited I/O bandwidth of the pins of conventionally packaged integrated circuits. It is expected that the bandwidth goal can be met with digital optics, as evidenced by the parallel sorting network design discussed in Chapter 5 which can serve as a packet sorter for a digital switch.

Historically, the speed of electronic digital computers has increased steadily due to improvements in device speed and packing density. Currently, inter-chip communication and heat dissipation limit further improvements in system speed, and there is little that can be done to solve these problems without creating novel approaches to system design. Where the speed of electronic circuits is limited by bandwidth, parallel processing may take up the slack. It is expected that parallel processing will account for processing speeds on the order of 100 to 1000 times greater than technology available in the 1980's [7], but all problems do not appear to be parallelizeable. Any computable function can be realized in two levels of logic given arbitrary fan-in and fan-out, but that applies only when all of the inputs are present at the same time. There is a causal relationship between events in the universe, and the time-ordered behavior of many processes cannot be expressed in a simple closed form. We will still rely on powerful sequential processors, augmented by parallelism where it can be effectively used. For this reason, a number of applications will need the switching bandwidth that digital optics can provide.

How much faster can computers run? Some estimates based on intraband switching transitions [121] indicate that optical switching speeds on the order of 50fs are attainable with present-day materials. Assuming that the supporting problems for 50fs operation are solvable, that would be an increase in operating speed of 10^4 over the fastest operating speeds currently attainable in an electronic digital computer. This is approximately equal to the amount of improvement in speed 1990 computers have over the early computers of the 1950's, so we are currently about halfway along the speed axis of a time/speed graph where 50fs switching is at the upper end. In terms of parallelism, we can expect improvement to the extent that the physical size of the machine limits overall performance. For the Connection Machine (CM) architecture parallelism in the form of 2^{16} one-bit processors arranged at the vertices of a 16-space hypercube increases system power by orders of magnitude (see Chapter 5). The CM architecture is extensible within physical limits to 2^{20} processors so we can expect that a great amount of improvement can be made in processing power through parallelism if other problems such as component failure and thermal dissipation can be solved.

We can gather from this discussion that the computing demands of some applications such as high bandwidth packet switching cannot be satisfied with current technology, and that the potential for digital optics to bridge the gap is great enough to justify working toward a future payoff from optical computing. VLSI and electronic GaAs are contending technologies that are fundamentally limited by packaging. It may be that electronic technology will be used for advanced machines that meet high bandwidth switching needs but only if packaging is handled differently, such as through optical components integrated with electronics on the same substrate. However it comes about, we can at least be certain that we do need faster computers and that we can create faster computers if radically new approaches are used, such as optical logic devices interconnected in free space with regular connection patterns.

Given that we need a new digital technology such as optical computing, the major ideas supported by the earlier chapters are summarized below.

We consider the use of optics in digital computing because electronic digital computing is limited to system speeds of a few hundred megahertz in its current form, whereas the expected operating rates of optical digital computers are on the order of 10's and 100's of gigahertz. Some limitations of electronics that contribute to the gigahertz barrier are [66]:

- Electromagnetic interference at high speed
- Edge transitions
- Complexity of metal connections
- Drive requirements for pins
- Large peak power levels
- Impedance matching effects

Some advantages of optics that allow the gigahertz barrier to be overcome are [66]:

- High connectivity through imaging
- No physical contact for interconnects
- Non-interference of signals
- High spatial and temporal bandwidth
- No feedback to the power source
- Inherently low signal dispersion

A recognized architecture for a digital optical computer supported throughout this book consists of arrays of optical logic devices interconnected in free space with regular interconnects. Optical signals travel orthogonal to the device substrates, and free space provides the connection medium. This allows for simple optical implementations without introducing significant complexity into the design process or the circuit breadth and depth of the target machine. A representation of this model is shown in Figure 6.1, where four stages of crossovers interconnect four arrays of optical logic devices. Unwanted connections are blocked with masks placed in the image planes.

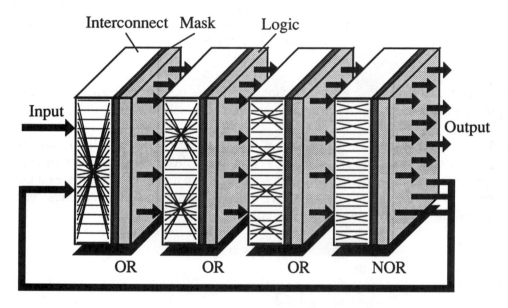

Figure 6.1: *Architectural model of a digital optical computer based on arrays of optical logic gates interconnected in free space with regular patterns.*

A four-stage implementation of this model using split+shift interconnects has been constructed at AT&T Bell Laboratories [97] as shown in Figure 6.2. The system is composed of four S-SEED arrays with an 8x4 matrix of NOR gates at the crosspoints of a Cartesian grid. Fan-in of the logic gates is two and fan-out is two. Operating speed reported in January, 1990 is one megahertz. The four modules occupy an area that is approximately 60cm x 60cm x 15cm. Although the speed and array size of this initial setup are not impressive when compared with electronics technology, both can be increased significantly without changing the underlying model of Figure 6.1. Gate density is limited primarily by fabrication parameters and field sizes of the lenses, and speed is limited primarily by available optical power from external lasers. These problems are not trivial, but do not pose any fundamental limitations either and gains are expected in the near future.

Figure 6.2: *An optical implementation of the model shown in Figure 6.1 is made up of four 4x8 arrays of S-SEED NOR gates and split+shift interconnects. Size is approximately 60cm x 60cm x 15cm deep. (Photograph provided by the courtesy of Nick Craft, AT&T Bell Laboratories.)*

Small circuits, on the order of four-variable PLAs, can be mapped onto this model in an algorithmic manner without making significant sacrifices in circuit depth or breadth. A random access memory can be mapped onto this structure that allows for arbitrarily large word width accesses, at a component count cost of less than two to three switching components per stored bit of information. The memory can be pipelined at the gate level so that throughput is limited by device speed rather than system speed. Tiling and partitioning are VLSI problems that also affect this model. However, the problems of tiling and partitioning are simplified as a result of the regular interconnection structure. Fault avoidance is simplified and is made more effective through simple techniques of array rotations, array exchanges, and circuit permutations. It is expected that fault recovery will be more extensive for optical computers based on this model because device arrays can be made usable once the failures are isolated, which may also be true for electronic digital systems but is considerably easier for the all-optical approach supported here (See Section 4.6). These insights provide evidence that this model is computationally powerful while addressing optical implementation details.

Three case studies are cited in Chapter 5: optical designs of a parallel sorting network, the Connection Machine, and a content addressable memory. Those examples are cited because they push electronics to its present limits, which can be extended through the use of optics. Good applications for free-space, digital optical computing can be characterized as requiring high throughput and high regular connectivity, and the Chapter 5 examples exploit these capabilities.

Circuits are customized in this model by blocking light in the image planes at selected locations. The same effect of enabling or disabling logic devices can be achieved by imaging arrays of control beams onto the arrays of devices as discussed in Chapter 4. The arrays of control beams can be obtained from storage loops, other optical computers, or the same optical computer. For these configurations, the entire connection pattern for the computer is changed on each time step, allowing for the potential of reusing hardware on the fly. The (space)×(time) product, which is commonly used for comparisons of parallel processing implementations, can be improved by reallocating unused hardware for some other purpose. It is suggested that this approach will allow a compiler to embed a novel machine description into the object code and that the resulting machine will be highly tuned for the problem at hand.

Currently, no real digital optical computers exist except for benchtype prototypes such as the implementation shown in Figure 6.2 so it is difficult to gauge the influence of optics in computing except for how optics can potentially affect current computing barriers. In this context, it is understood that speed is the one desirable attribute of next-generation computers that more money simply will not buy. Size and bandwidth for the most part can be satisfied for a price. The position supported in this book is that high speed digital optical computers will be made possible by maintaining a regular structure in the hardware and by maintaining simplicity in the design methods. Those are the two, most important ideas supported in this text, in an effort to advance the long range progress of the field of digital optical computing.

Bibliography

1. Abu-Mostafa, Y. S. and D. Psaltis, "Optical neural computers," *Scientific American*, **256**, 88, (1987).

2. Ambekar, S. M., W. E. Hamilton and T. E. Cole, "Systems Packaging," *AT&T Technical Journal*, **66,** (4), 81, (1987).

3. Arrathoon, R., "Digital optical computing," *Proc. SPIE*, **752**, (Jan. 1987).

4. Athale, R. A., "Optical matrix algebraic processors: a survey," *IEEE 1983 International Optical Computing Conference*, H. J. Caulfield, ed., 24, (1983).

5. Athale, R. A., "Optical implementations of neural computing," *Optical Computing*, (1989 Technical Digest Series, Optical Society of America, Washington, D.C.), **9**, 2, (1989).

6. Bell, T. E., "Optical computing: a field in flux," *IEEE Spectrum*, 34, (Aug. 1986).

7. Bernhard, R., "Computing at the speed limit," *IEEE Spectrum*, (Mar. 1982).

8. Botha, E., D. Casasent and E. Barnard, "Optical symbolic substitution using multi-channel correlators," *Appl. Opt.*, **27**, 817, (Mar. 1, 1988).

9. Brenner, K.-H., "New implementation of symbolic substitution logic," *Appl. Opt.*, **25**, 3061, (1986).

10. Brenner, K.-H. and A. Huang, "Optical implementation of the perfect shuffle interconnections," *Appl. Opt.*, **27**, 135, (1988).

11.   Brenner, K.-H., A. Huang and N. Streibl, "Digital optical computing with symbolic substitution," *Appl. Opt.*, **25**, 3054, (1986).

12.   Burks, A. W., *Essays on Cellular Automata*, University of Illinois Press, (1970).

13.   Casasent, D. and A. Ghosh, "Optical linear algebra.," *SPIE*, **388**, G. Michael Morris, ed., 182, (1983).

14.   Cloonan, T. J., "Optical data manipulator network," unpublished manuscript, (1987).

15.   Cloonan, T. J. and F. B. McCormick, private communication, (1987).

16.   Codd, E. F., *Cellular Automata*, Academic Press, (1968).

17.   Cooley, J. W. and J. W. Tukey, "An algorithm for the machine calculation of complex Fourier series," *Math. Comp.*, **19**, 297, (1965).

18.   Craft, N. C. and M. E. Prise, "Optical systems tolerances for symmetric self electrooptic effect devices in optical computers," *Optical Computing*, **9**, (1989 Technical Digest Series, Optical Society of America, Washington, D. C.), 334, (1989).

19.   Cutrona, L. J., E. N. Leith, L. J. Porcello and W. E. Vivian, "On the application of coherent processing techniques to synthetic aperture radar," *Proc. IEEE*, **54**, 1026, (1966).

20.   Davidson, E. S., "An algorithm for NAND decomposition under network constraints," *IEEE Trans. Comp.*, **C-18,** (12), 1098, (1979).

21.   Domash, L. H. and M. Cronin-Golomb, "Cellular Automaton Computation with Nonlinear Optics," *Twenty-Third Asilomar Conference on Signals, Systems & Computers*, **1**, 106, (1989).

22.   Douglass, R. J., "A day in the life of a new-generation computer user," Next-Generation Computers, IEEE Press, 46, (1985).

23.   Eichmann, G. and Y. Li, "Compact optical generalized perfect shuffle," *Appl. Opt.*, **26,** (7), 1167, (1987).

24. Ersoy, O. K., "Electrooptical processing of signal transforms," *Appl. Opt.*, **26**, 676, (Feb. 15, 1987).

25. Feitelson, D., *Optical Computing*, The MIT Press, (1988).

26. Feng, T.-Y., "A survey of interconnection networks," *IEEE Computer*, 12, (Dec. 1981).

27. Foster, C. C., *Content Addressable Parallel Processors*, Van Nostrand Reinhold Company, (1976).

28. Franklin, M. A., D. F. Wann and W. J. Thomas, "Pin limitations and partitioning of VLSI interconnection networks," *IEEE Trans. Comp.*, **C-31**, 1109, (Nov. 1982).

29. Garner, H. L., "The residue number system," *IRE Trans. Elec. Comp.*, **8**, 140, (Jun. 1959).

30. Gibbs, H. M., *Optical Bistability: Controlling Light with Light*, Academic Press, (1985).

31. Gibbs, H. M., P. Mandel, N. Peyghambarian and S. D. Smith, *Optical Bistability III: Proceedings of the Topical Meeting*, Proceedings in Physics 8, (1985).

32. Gibbs, H. M. and N. Peyghambarian, "Nonlinear etalons and optical computing," *Optical and Hybrid Computing*, **634**, 142, (1987).

33. Gindi, G. R., A. F. Gmitro and K. Parthasarathy, "Hopfield model associative memory with nonzero-diagonal terms in memory matrix," *Appl. Opt.*, **26**, 261, (Jan. 15, 1987).

34. Goodman, J. W., *Introduction to Fourier Optics*, McGraw-Hill Book Co., (1968).

35. Goodman, J. W., "Optical computing, an historical perspective," *IEEE CH2135-2/85*, 282, (1985).

36. Goodman, J. W., F. I. Leonberger, S.-Y. Kung and R. A. Athale, "Optical interconnections for VLSI systems," *Proc. IEEE*, **72**, 850, (Jul. 1984).

37. Guilfoyle, P. S. and W. J. Wiley, "Combinatorial logic based digital optical computing architectures," *Appl. Opt.*, **27**, 1661, (May 1, 1988).

38. Guilfoyle, P. S. and F. F. Zeise, "Reconfigurable programmable optical digital computer," *Optical Computing*, **9**, 366, (1989).

39. Hall, J. S., S. Levy and M. J. Murdocca, "Design of an optical Connection Machine," *AIAA Computers in Aerospace VI Conference*, 195, (1987).

40. Haney, M. and D. Psaltis, "Real-time programmable acoustooptic synthetic aperture radar processor," *Appl. Opt.*, **27**, 1786, (May 1, 1988).

41. Håstad, J. T., *Computational Limitations for Small-Depth Circuits*, The MIT Press, (1987).

42. Hill, F. J. and G. R. Peterson, *Digital Systems: Hardware Organization and Design*, John Wiley & Sons, (1978).

43. Hillis, W. D., "New computer architectures and their relationship to physics or Why computer science is no good," *Int. J. Theo. Phys.*, **21**(3/4), 255, (1982).

44. Hillis, W. D., "The Connection Machine: A computer architecture based on cellular automata," *Cellular Automata: Proceedings of an Interdisciplinary Workshop*, Physica 10D, Los Alamos, NM, (1984).

45. Hillis, W. D., *The Connection Machine*, The MIT Press, (1985).

46. Hinton, H. S., "Photonic switching technology applications," *AT&T Tech. J.*, **66,** (3), 41, (1987).

47. Howard, J. N., ed., "Optical Artificial Intelligence," *Appl. Opt.*, **26**, (May 15, 1987).

48. Huang, A., "Design for an optical general purpose digital computer," *SPIE 1980 International Optical Computing Conference*, W. T. Rhodes, ed., (1980).

49. Huang, A., "Parallel algorithms for optical digital computers," *IEEE 1983 10th International Optical Computing Conference*, H. J. Caulfield, ed., Cambridge, MA. (1983).

50. Huang, A., "Architectural considerations involved in the design of an optical digital computer," *Proc. IEEE*, **72**, 780, (1984).

51. Huang, A., "Impact of new technological advances and architectural insights on the design of optical computers," *Proc. SPIE*, J. A. Neff, ed., (1984).

52. Huang, A., "Computational origami - the folding of circuits and systems," *Optical Computing, 1989 Technical Digest Series*, **9**, 198, (1989).

53. Huang, A. and J. W. Goodman, "Number theoretic processors, optical and electronic," *SPIE Optical Processing Systems*, (1979).

54. Huang, A. and S. Knauer, "Starlite: A wideband digital switch," *GLOBECOM '84*, IEEE 84CH2064-4, (Nov. 1984).

55. Huang, A., Y. Tsunoda, J. W. Goodman and S. Ishihara, "Optical computation using residue arithmetic," *Appl. Opt.*, **18**, 149, (Jan. 18, 1979).

56. Huang, K. S., B. K. Jenkins and A. A. Sawchuk, "Binary Image Algebra and Digital Optical Cellular Image Processors," *Topical Meeting on Optical Computing*, **11**, (1987 Technical Digest Series, Optical Society of America, Washington, D.C.), 20, (1987).

57. Hwang, K. and F. A. Briggs, *Computer Architectures and Parallel Processing*, McGraw-Hill, (1984).

58. Texas Instruments, *The TTL Data Book for Design Engineers*, Texas Instruments, Inc., (1976).

59. Jahns, J., "Efficient Hadamard transformation of large images," *Signal Processing 5*, North-Holland Publishing, (1983).

60. Jahns, J. and M. J. Murdocca, "Crossover networks and their optical implementation," *Appl. Opt.*, **27**, (15), 3155, (1988).

61. Jeon, H.-I. and A. A. Sawchuk, "Optical crossbar interconnections using variable grating mode devices," *Appl. Opt.*, **26**, 261, (Jan. 15, 1987).

62. Jewell, J. L., M. J. Murdocca, S. L. McCall, Y. H. Lee and A. Scherer, "Digital Optical Computing: Devices, Systems, Architectures," *Proceedings of The Seventh International Conference on Integrated Optics and Optical Fiber Communication*, Kobe, Japan, (Jul. 18, 1989).

63. Jewell, J. L., A. Scherer, S. L. McCall, A. C. Gossard and J. H. English, "GaAs-AlAs monolithic microresonator arrays," *Appl. Phys. Lett.*, **51,** (2), 94, (Jul. 13, 1987).

64. Jewell, J. L., A. Scherer, S. L. McCall, Y. H. Lee, S. J. Walker, J. P. Harbison and L. T. Florez, "Low threshold electrically-pumped vertical cavity surface-emitting microlasers," *Electron. Lett.*, **25**, 1123, (1989).

65. Johnson, J. L., "Architectural relationships involving symbolic substitution," *Appl. Opt.*, **27**, 529, (Feb. 1, 1987).

66. Jordan, H. F., "Report of the workshop on all-optical, stored program, digital computers," Technical Report, Department of Electrical and Computer Engineering, University of Colorado at Boulder, (1988).

67. Jordan, H. F., "A Bit Serial Optical Computer," *Topical Meeting on Optical Computing*, **11**, (1987 Technical Digest Series, Optical Society of America, Washington, D.C.), 24, (1987).

68. Kahn, A. H. and U. R. Nejib., "Optical logic gates employing liquid crystal optical switches," *Appl. Opt.*, **26**, 270, (Jan. 15, 1987).

69. Keyes, R. W. and J. A. Armstrong, "Thermal limitations in optical logic," *Appl. Opt.*, **8**, 2549, (Dec. 1969).

70. Knuth, D., *The Art of Computer Programming*, Addison Wesley, (1973).

71. Lang, T. and H. S. Stone, "A shuffle-exchange network with simplified control," *IEEE Trans. Comp.*, **C-25,** (1), 55, (1976).

72. Langton, C. G., "Self-reproduction in cellular automata," Physica 10D, 135, (1984).

73. Lawrie, D. H., "Access and alignment of data in an array processor," *IEEE Trans. Comp.*, **C-24**, (12), 1145, (1975).

74. Lee, J. N., "Optical and acousto-optical techniques in radar and sonar," *Optical Computing*, J. A. Neff, ed., (1984).

75. Lee, S. H., S. C. Esener, M. A. Title and T. J. Drabik, "Two-dimensional Si/PLZT light modulators: design considerations and technology," *Opt. Eng.*, **23**, 250, (1986).

76. Lentine, A. L., H. S. Hinton, D. A. B. Miller, J. E. Henry, J. E. Cunningham and L. M. F. Chirovsky, "The symmetric self electro-optic effect device," *Conference on Lasers and Electro-optics*, **14**, 249, (1987).

77. Li, Y. and G. Eichmann, "Conditional symbolic modified signed digit arithmetic using optical content-addressable memory logic elements," *Appl. Opt.*, **25**, (10), 1530, (Jun. 15, 1987).

78. Macukow, B. and H. H. Arsenault, "Optical associative memory model based on neural networks having variable interconnection weights," *Appl. Opt.*, **26**, 924, (Mar. 1, 1987).

79. Mait, J. N. and K.-H. Brenner, "Optical systems for symbolic substitution," *Topical Meeting on Optical Computing*, (Technical Digest Series 1987, Optical Society of America, Washington, D.C.), **11**, 12-15, (1987).

80. Mead, C. and L. Conway, *Introduction to VLSI Systems*, Addison Wesley, (1980).

81. Midwinter, J. E., "A novel approach to the design of optically activated wideband switching matrices," *Proc. IEE*, Part J, Opto-electronics, to appear.

82. Miller, D. A. B., D. S. Chemla, T. C. Damen, T. H. Wood, C. A. Burrus, A. C. Gossard and W. Wiegmann, "The quantum well self-electrooptic effect device: optoelectronic bistability and oscillation and self-linearized modulation," *IEEE J. Quant. Electron*, **QE-21**, 1462, (1985).

83.   Mirsalehi, M. M. and T. K. Gaylord, "Residue number system in content-addressable memory processors," *Digital Optical Computing*, **752**, R. Arrathoon, ed., 175, (1987).

84.   Morenoff, E., W. Beckett, P. G. Kesel, F. J. Winninghoff and P. M. Wolff, "4-way parallel processor partition of an atmospheric primitive-equation prediction model," *Spring Joint Computer Conference*, **38**, 39, (1971).

85.   Murdocca, M. J., *Techniques for Parallel Numeric and Non-numeric Algorithm Design in Digital Optics*, Master's Thesis, Department of Computer Science, Rutgers University at New Brunswick, (1985).

86.   Murdocca, M. J., "Digital optical computing with one-rule cellular automata," *Appl. Opt.*, **26**, 3365, (1987).

87.   Murdocca, M. J., "Proposal for an optical content-addressable memory," *Optical Computing*, **9**, 210, (1989).

88.   Murdocca, M. J. and T. Cloonan, "Optical design of a digital switch," *Appl. Opt.*, **28**, 2505, (Jul. 1, 1989).

89.   Murdocca, M. J. and A. Huang, "Symbolic substitution methods for optical computing," *Optical Computing 88*, **963**, 585, (1988).

90.   Murdocca, M. J. and B. Sugla, "Design of a symbolic substitution based, optical random access memory," *Optical Computing*, **9**, (1989 Technical Digest Series, Optical Society of America, Washington, D.C.), 92, (1989).

91.   Murdocca, M. J. and B. Sugla, "Design for an optical random access memory," *Appl. Opt.*, **28**, 182, (Jan. 1, 1989).

92.   O'Neill, J., unpublished work, (1983).

93.   Parker, D. S. Jr., "Notes on shuffle / exchange-type switching networks," *IEEE Trans. Comp.*, **C-29**, (3), 213, (1980).

94.   Poirier, J. C., "EXCELLERATOR: Automated leaf cell layout agent," *IEEE International Conference on Computer Aided Design*, 176, (1987).

95. Pradhan, D. K., *Fault-Tolerant Computing I*, Prentice-Hall, 344-347, (1986).

96. Premkumar, U. V. and J. C. Browne, "Resource allocation in rectangular SW banyans," *The Proceedings of the 9th Annual Symposium on Computer Architecture*, 326, (1982).

97. Prise, M. E., "Optical computing using self electro-optic effect devices," SPIE *O-E/Lase '90*, **1214**, (1990).

98. Prise, M. E., N. Streibl and M. M. Downs, "Computational properties of nonlinear optical devices," *Topical Meeting on Photonic Switching*, (Technical Digest Series 1987, Optical Society of America, Washington, D.C.), **11**, 110, (1987).

99. Psaltis, D., D. Brady and K. Wagner, "Adaptive optical networks using photorefractive crystals," *Appl. Opt.*, **27**, 1752, (May 1, 1988).

100. Quinn, M. J., *Designing Efficient Algorithms for Parallel Computers*, McGraw-Hill, (1987).

101. Rajbenbach, H., Y. Fainman and S. H. Lee, "Optical implementation of an iterative algorithm for matrix inversion," *Appl. Opt.*, **26**, 1024, (Mar. 15, 1987).

102. Rhodes, W. T., "Acousto-optic signal processing: convolution and correlation," *Proc. IEEE*, **69**, 65, (1981).

103. Rhodes, W. T., "Optical signal processing: Fourier transforms and convolution / correlation," *Optical and Hybrid Computing*, **634**, 57, (1987).

104. Rhodes, W. T., Special issue on neural networks, *Appl. Opt.*, **26**, (Dec. 1, 1987).

105. Russell, R. M., "The CRAY-1 computer system," *Comm. ACM*, **21**, 63, (Jan. 1978).

106. Sawchuk, A. A., "Digital logic and computing with optics," *Optical Computing*, **456**, 41, (1984).

107. Schaefer, D. H. and J. P. Strong III, "Tse Computers," *Proc. IEEE*, **65**, 129, (Jan. 1977).

108. Siegel, H. J., "Interconnection networks for SIMD machines," *IEEE Computer*, **12**, 57, (Jun. 1979).

109. Siegel, H. J., "The theory underlying the partitioning of permutation networks," *IEEE Trans. Comp.*, **C-29**, 791, (Sep. 1980).

110. Smith, S. D., A. C. Walker, F. A. P. Tooley and B. S. Wherrett, "The demonstration of restoring digital optical logic," *Nature*, **325**, 27, (Jan. 1, 1987).

111. Smith, S. D., A. C. Walker, B. S. Wherrett and F. A. P. Tooley, "Prospects for optically bistable devices in digital optical circuits for a simple optical finite state machine," *Optical and Hybrid Computing*, **634**, 134, (1987).

112. Stirk, C. W. and R. A. Athale, "Sorting with optical compare-and-exchange modules," *Appl. Opt.*, **27**, 1721, (May 1, 1988).

113. Stirk, C. W., R. A. Athale and C. B. Friedlander, "Optical implementation of the compare-and-exchange operation for applications in symbolic computing," *SPIE Optical and Digital Pattern Recognition*, **754**, 175, (1987).

114. Stone, H. S., "Parallel processing with the perfect shuffle," *IEEE Trans. Comp.*, **C-20**, (2), 153, (1971).

115. Sugla, B., "Computing on a digital optical computer using regular interconnections," *SPIE Optical Computing 88*, **963**, J. W. Goodman, P. Chavel, G. Roblin, eds., 668, (1988).

116. Tanida, J. and Y. Ichioka, "Optical logic array processor," *IEEE 1983 10th International Optical Computing Conference*, 18, (1983).

117. Toffoli, T. and N. Margolus, *Cellular Automata Machines*, The MIT Press, (1987).

118. Von Neumann, J., "Nonlinear capacitance or inductance switching, amplifying and memory devices," *John von Neumann's Collected Works*, MacMillan, (1963).

119. Wang, L., H. M. Chou, H. M. Gibbs, G. C. Giglioli, G. Khitrova, H.-M. Kulcke, R. Jin, H. A. Macleod, N. Peyghambarian, R. W. Sprague and M. T. Tsao, "Symbolic substitution using ZnS interference filters," *SPIE Digital Optical Computing*, **752**, R. Arrathoon, ed., 14, (1987).

120. West, L. C., *Spectroscopy of GaAs Quantum Wells*, Ph.D. dissertation, Stanford University, (1985).

121. West, L. C., personal communication, (1988).

122. West, L. C., "Picosecond integrated optical logic," *IEEE Computer*, 34, (Dec. 1987).

123. Wherrett, B. S., "All-optical computation: a design for tackling a specific physical problem," *Appl. Opt.*, **24**, 2876, (1985).

124. Wolfram, S., *Theory and Applications of Cellular Automata*, World Scientific, (1986).

125. Wu, C.-L. and T.-Y. Feng, "The universality of the shuffle-exchange network," *IEEE Trans. Comp.*, **C-30,** (5), 324, (1981).

126. Yatagai, T., "Optical cellular logic computers and space-variant logic gate array," *Optical and Hybrid Computing*, **634**, 157, (1987).

127. Yeh, P., A. Chiou and J. Hong, "Optical interconnection using photorefractive dynamic holograms," *Appl. Opt.*, **27**, 2093, (1988).

Index

The MIT Press, with Peter Denning as general consulting editor, publishes computer science books in the following series:

ACM Doctoral Dissertation Award and Distinguished Dissertation Series

Artificial Intelligence
Patrick Winston, founding editor
J. Michael Brady, Daniel G. Bobrow, and Randall Davis, editors

Charles Babbage Institute Reprint Series for the History of Computing
Martin Campbell-Kelly, editor

Computer Systems
Herb Schwetman, editor

Explorations with Logo
E. Paul Goldenberg, editor

Foundations of Computing
Michael Garey and Albert Meyer, editors

History of Computing
I. Bernard Cohen and William Aspray, editors

Information Systems
Michael Lesk, editor

Logic Programming
Ehud Shapiro, editor; Koichi Furukawa, Fernando Pereira, and David H. D. Warren, associate editors

The MIT Press Electrical Engineering and Computer Science Series

Research Monographs in Parallel and Distributed Processing
Christopher Jesshope and David Klappholz, editors

Scientific and Engineering Computation
Janusz Kowalik, editor

Technical Communication
Ed Barrett, editor